Planning Guide
for the Beginning Retailer

Planning Guide

for the Beginning Retailer

Albert Smart

RETAILING FOR PROFIT SERIES

Lebhar-Friedman Books
Chain Store Publishing Corp.
A Subsidiary of Lebhar-Friedman, Inc.
New York

Planning Guide for the Beginning Retailer
Retailing for Profit Series

Copyright © 1980, Chain Store Publishing Corp.
425 Park Avenue, New York, N.Y. 10022

Printed in the United States of America

Library of Congress Cataloging in Publication Data

Smart, Albert
    Planning Guide for the Beginning Retailer

    (Retailing for Profit Series)
    1. Retail Trade—Management.   I. Title
II. Series.
HF5429.S573   658.8'7   79-25510
ISBN 0-912016-85-X

5 4 3 2 1

I wish to acknowledge
Professor Richard Howland
of Northern Illinois University's
Marketing Department, who read the
manuscript, and all my other colleagues
and friends who offered encouragement and
motivation during the preparation of this manual.

Contents

Preface

Retailing today is characterized by increased competition, rising expenses, and tighter profits. It is a field that is relatively easy to enter; it does not require excessive amounts of capital funds as compared with the capital funds needed to enter other areas of business. Small- and medium-sized merchants typically have limited training and experience, but numerically they dominate the retailing community. There is an acute need for retailers to become more knowledgeable about the field so that they are able to merchandise their goods and services more efficiently and profitably.

Professor Smart's book provides the retailer with valuable information. It helps to familiarize the reader with some of the key elements of retailing. It has been written especially for the beginning retailer who needs to be better informed about basic retailing. The author covers the key elements of retailing from the practitioner's perspective in a clear and understandable fashion.

A book like the *Planning Guide for the Beginnning Retailer*, aimed at the novice retailer, is long overdue. It should prove invaluable to those who seek to do a better job of merchandising their store and analyzing the results of operations.

Richard H. Howland
Professor of Marketing and
    former Department Chairman
Northern Illinois University
DeKalb, Illinois

Introduction

Planning is a prerequisite of successful retailing. Without it the retailer will not be able to attain desired goals and objectives. Planning, be it short- or long-range, is one of the most important tasks the beginning retailer will undertake in operating the store. It covers a broad range of activities, but it is basically concerned with identifying *what* functions are to be performed in the operation of the store, deciding *who* will perform the functions, and setting dates as to *when* the functions should be completed. In planning, the object is to make a good decision which will result in the right action at the right time.

This book is divided into seven chapters. Chapter One, "Planning and Controlling the Stock," presents methods which the beginning retailer can use to plan and control inventories. It also advises the retailer on how to plan which stocks to carry based on the various sources of product information.

Chapter Two, "Planning the Cash Flow," points out and explains that the beginning retailer needs adequate funds to meet operating costs (such as cash receipts and cash disbursements).

Chapter Three, "Planning the Interior Layout of the Store," stresses the importance of store atmospherics. The selling methods to be used, as well as the arrangement of fixtures, equipment, and merchandise within the store are all discussed.

Chapter Four, "Planning the Pricing Strategy," focuses on price setting and price adjusting, including markups and markdowns. Special pricing situations, such as leader pricing and even-odd pricing, are also covered in this chapter.

Chapter Five, "Planning the Advertising and Promotional Strategy," is concerned with how a store reaches out to attract and appeal to its target customers via media communication. It shows how advertising and various kinds of promotional methods can be employed to reach potential customers.

Chapter Six, "Planning and Controlling Operating Expenses," explains expense budgeting, expense classification, and methods of allocating expenses to the various revenue-producing departments of the store.

Finally, Chapter Seven, "Other Planning Elements," gives some insights into planning such elements as customer services, profits, retail reductions, sales, and purchases.

Other books which are planned for this series include: (1) *Retail Merchandising and Control,* (2) *Retailing Expenses and Productivity,* (3) *Retail Pricing Policies and Procedures,* (4) *Retail Sales Promotion: The Communication Problem,* and (5) *Franchising.*

Chapter One

PLANNING AND CONTROLLING THE STOCK

The proper planning of the composition of the stock is a prerequisite of unit stock control, and it helps the retail merchant to make a proper determination of the extent of stock depth and breadth. Planning the stock also helps the beginning merchant to achieve the desired balance between the size of the merchandise inventory and sales.

By inspecting the stock and studying records, the small retail merchant can achieve the desired relationship between stocks and sales. As the size of the assortment increases, maintaining a balanced stock condition becomes increasingly more difficult. It becomes less practical for the proprietor to personally inspect the merchandise, and more records of various types must be kept as a basis for making sound decisions. These records are an integral part of the overall control of the merchandise.

The general objective of merchandise management or control is to provide merchandise assortments which meet the needs and wants of target customers. In order to achieve this balanced stock condition, the retail merchant needs to develop a system which will provide information concerning what, when, and how much stock to buy for the store. Obtaining and using this kind of information helps make control possible.

Once the merchant has achieved the basic objective of merchandise control—a balanced stock condition—other specific goals of merchandise management can be sought.

One specific goal or objective of a retail merchant is to meet customers' needs and wants adequately. As an intermediary between suppliers and consumers, the retail merchant should provide the goods that customers want, at prices they think are fair and which they are willing to pay. Proper merchandise control will help the merchant to attain this goal.

A second specific objective of the retail merchant is to sell merchandise at a profit. Balanced stock conditions lead to greater sales and fewer markdowns; accordingly, the gross profit margin is increased. If the merchant is able to prevent operating expenses from rising proportionately, net profit will also increase. Other things which will help improve profits include a careful monitoring of stock to detect early the slow- and fast-moving items so that the slow sellers can be minimized; to keep stock *clean* and *fresh* which tends to make it more saleable; and to emphasize advertising and sales promotional efforts to help generate sales.

A third specific objective of the retail merchant should be to keep the investment in stock at an optimal or adequate level to meet customer demand. This, of course, would lead to an improved stock turnover condition. It should also result in an improved rate of return on the funds invested in the inventory.

Merchandise Assortment Needs

In preparation for planning the merchandise assortment needs of the store, the beginning retail merchant should consider who the desired customers are—the key target market of the store. The merchant should gear all of the merchandising efforts of the store, including buying for the store, pricing, displaying, promoting, and providing services, toward attracting this target market, be it a luxury, budget, suburban, inner-city, or youth market. In addition, the merchandising policies of the store should be consistent with the kind of store image the beginning merchant desires to create and cultivate. For example, a shoe store merchant will not want to stock high-priced, brand-name shoes if the store is attempting to attract a working class target group. This would be inconsistent with a low price policy.

Once the retail merchant has decided what merchandise to buy, then the composition of that stock, in terms of the quality and the number of sizes, colors, styles, and brands, should be decided on. At the outset, the merchant may not wish to stock an excessive quantity of brands or styles, because this will inevitably increase the amount of capital funds that would be tied up in merchandise which may be selling or turning over slowly. Of course, the merchandise assortment, including depth, breadth, and consistency, can be varied over time at the discretion of the proprietor. These characteristics of the merchandise assortment are discussed in the following pages.

Depth of Assortment. Merchandise assortments differ in the extent of their depth. Depth as used here refers to the number of brands and/or styles within a given product category that a retail merchant carries in stock. For example, Supermarket A may carry in its Health and Beauty Aids section five to ten different types of hand lotion, while Supermarket B stocks a selection of twenty to thirty different types. These two retail establishments differ in the depth of assortment of hand lotions they carry in stock. More specifically, Supermarket B has considerably greater depth than Supermarket A. Even though Supermarket A, with five to ten brands, will satisfy the needs of a smaller number of hand lotion users, it will have considerably less capital funds tied up in hand lotion inventory than Supermarket B.

Breadth of Assortment. The breadth of assortment refers to the number of different classes of products a merchant carries in stock. For example, Mac's Sporting Goods Store sells only shoes and clothing, while Taylor's Sporting Goods Store stocks hunting equipment, boats, golfing equipment, and bowling equipment in addition to shoes and clothing. Taylor's features more breadth or a wider line than Mac's. Similar to increasing the amount of depth, increasing the extent of breadth would require a larger investment in inventories. However, with more breadth the merchant would be able to satisfy the needs and wants of a larger number of customers.

The importance of depth and breadth to the beginning merchant is illustrated by the following examples. Sue's Specialty Shop carries only two product lines in stock. Product line I is comprised of ten different brands or styles, while product line II features only four brands or styles. The average depth (the total number of brands or styles divided by the number of lines) would be seven (14 ÷ 2). The Tinker Specialty Shop carries five product lines in stock. Product line I is comprised of five brands or styles; product line II, twelve brands or styles; product line III, four brands or styles, product line IV, six brands or styles; and product line V, eight brands or styles. In this store, the average depth is also seven (35 ÷ 5). Since there are, however, five product lines in Tinker's store and thirty-five brands or styles, its assortment is considerably more extensive than Sue's store which carries only two product lines and fourteen brands or styles in stock.

Even though specialty stores by their nature tend to carry relatively few lines in stock, they can have attractive assortments by emphasizing more depth. In contrast, the typical variety store will feature numerous different lines, usually at the expense of depth. The department store or discount mass merchandise merchant tends to emphasize both depth and breadth of merchandise assortment.

Consistency in the Assortment. A third dimension of the assortment is consistency, which is the extent to which the merchandise comprising the assortment is related. If all of the merchandise carried by a store is related in use, the assortments are consistent. For example, if a store which sells office supplies and equipment also carries typewriters and writing paper it would be reflecting consistency in the assortment. On the other hand, if the office supply and equipment store also carried some soft goods, it would have an inconsistent merchandise assortment.

Open-to-Buy

The open-to-buy is the dollar value of merchandise a merchant is to receive into stock during a given planning period. It is a method of regulating the merchandise purchases for a period of time such as six months, three months, or one month. When using the open-to-buy system, a record is maintained of all orders placed with suppliers for delivery during each month, and these orders are charged against the total planned purchases for the period. Whenever the information is desired during the planning period (perhaps once a week), a report can be prepared which shows the total of the purchase commitments to date and the remaining amount in the purchase account which is still unspent. The unspent balance constitutes the current open-to-buy.

The open-to-buy is especially useful when a merchant wants to know the status of the stock in the middle of a planning period. A simple open-to-buy account is presented below.

Open-To-Buy Account
(Month of March)

Planned purchases for March	$10,000
Amount of orders placed by the end of the first week in March	2,000
Current open-to-buy	$ 8,000
Goods on order March 1 and received into stock by the end of the second week in March	$ 3,000
Current open-to-buy	$ 5,000

As long as no orders have been placed to satisfy the planned purchases for March, open-to-buy is $10,000, the same as planned purchases for March. If at the end of the first week in March, orders in the amount of $2,000 were placed but no goods received into stock, current open-to-buy would amount to $8,000. If orders in the amount of $3,000 to satisfy the purchase requirements were placed by March 1 and received by the end of the second week in March, the open-to-buy would be $5,000.

There are several factors that affect the amount of merchandise a merchant is *open-to-buy* during a given planning period. The process of calculating the open-to-buy usually starts with *planned purchases*. The factors needed to determine planned purchases are (1) planned sales, (2) beginning of the month inventory, (3) planned end of the month inventory, and (4) planned reductions for the month. The equation for calculating the planned purchases figure for the month is:

Planned purchases = planned sales + planned reductions
+ planned end of month inventory
− beginning of month inventory

Assume planned sales are $6,000, planned reductions are $500, planned end of month inventory is $12,000, and beginning of month inventory, $10,000. Substituting in the above equation, planned purchases for the month are $8,500.

Planned purchases = $6,000 + 500 + 12,000 − 10,000
= $8,500

After the planned purchases are known, the open-to-buy is calculated by starting with the planned purchases figure, and deducting the merchandise received to date and merchandise on order to be received during the month. Assume the merchandise received to date is valued at $3,000 (retail), and the merchandise on order for delivery during the month is set at $1,000 (retail). Then, the open-to-buy can be calculated as follows:

Open to buy = planned purchases − merchandise received
− merchandise on order for delivery during month

Substituting in the above equation,

$$\text{Open to buy} = \$8,500 - 3,000 - 1,000$$
$$= \$4,500$$

The \$4,500 is the current amount of the open-to-buy at retail value. The cost equivalent depends on the markup percentage used. If the markup is 40 percent of retail, the cost equivalent would be \$2,700 [\$4,500 × (100% − 40%)].

It is advisable to maintain some open-to-buy during much of the planning period for several reasons. First, there is a stream of new products continually coming from the wholesale market. To be able to buy some of the fresh merchandise helps the merchant to maintain customer interest in the store's offerings, and it helps the store to increase its sales and profit. Second, if the purchase limit is open, it is possible to take advantage of special prices and other concessions that might be offered by suppliers. Finally, if an open-to-buy exists, the merchant can buy *fill-in* merchandise which may be necessary if a complete assortment is to be maintained.

Planning What Brands to Carry, Sources of Information

The beginning retail merchant must decide what brands or styles to carry in the store to meet the needs and wants of target customers. Because of the numerous products available in the market, choosing which brands to stock is not an easy job. The decision about which items to purchase and in what quantities depends upon the available information concerning the types, kinds, and prices of goods offered by suppliers and upon what the potential customers want.

A good starting point in deciding what to inventory is to determine a general product type. Are you going to sell soft or durable goods? The answer to this question must be decided before proceeding further. Once the decision is made to carry durable goods, for example, the second-level decision, concerning what line of durables to carry in stock, follows. This decision may be to carry only major appliances and television sets. After making the primary and secondary decisions concerning what merchandise to inventory, the decision as to what specific kinds comes next. This decision involves selecting the brands, sizes, colors, and materials.

At this stage of decision-making, there are some constraints which must be considered. Among these are the availability of funds for buying, the prices of the proposed merchandise, and the potential demand for the merchandise under consideration. Limited funds, high suppliers' prices, and low consumer demand are definite buying constraints for a proposed store.

Once the decisions as to what specific products to inventory are made, the beginning retail merchant needs to know what the available sources of product information are. Among the important sources of information are vendors, market representatives, customer surveys, trade papers, newspapers, and general publications.

Vendors' Offerings. The offerings of vendors can be a valuable source of merchandise information for the beginning retailer and a reliable guide for store buyers as well, especially if the vendors are keeping current about what consumers want.

Some vendors use salespersons to keep retail merchants informed as to what products are selling. Others may use periodic reports or bulletins, particularly in the case of fashion merchandise, to keep their clients informed. These should be carefully evaluated because some vendors tend to be concerned only about what they are producing or distributing rather than with what consumers want. Because of this possibility, several different sources should be evaluated before making a decision on what merchandise to buy from suppliers.

Market Representatives. Market representatives are a second source of product information. They act mainly as guides or aides to the retail merchant. Market representatives supply merchants with valuable market information about the availability of merchandise. They usually have offices in central markets (such as New York City, in the case of apparels) and are quite helpful to the smaller specialty merchant. Market representatives are knowledgeable concerning vendors' offerings. They carefully observe fashion trends and keep current on promotions in large city stores. They compile statistical reports on their findings and transmit these to store buyers through bulletins, or verbally when the store buyers visit the central market.

Customer Surveys. Surveying prospective customers is another way of obtaining information about what products to carry. A questionnaire is one type of survey technique that can be used to collect information concerning the needs and wants of consumers. In the questionnaire, target customers are asked what types, colors, and price ranges of merchandise they would prefer. The results are tabulated and summarized for use. The questionnaire may be mailed to people selected for the sample, or it may be filled in through personal interviews.

Another type of survey which is used principally by merchants who sell fashion goods is called the *style count*. Basically, the style count is conducted by placing observers at certain points and having them note what type of clothing people are wearing. The observation points should be carefully chosen to ensure that a broad spectrum of consumers are represented. The style count method of surveying consumers is also a valuable source of information for stores or departments selling fashion merchandise.

Trade Papers, Newspapers, and General Publications. The beginning merchant can get helpful, current information concerning what target customers want from trade magazines, fashion magazines, and newspapers. Merchants who sell women's wear can get valuable insights from publications such as *Vogue, Harper's Bazaar, Mademoiselle,* and *Women's Wear Daily.* These magazines show and discuss some of the latest fashion items. Retail merchants who feature men's wear can obtain information on what is current in such magazines as *Gentlemen's Quarterly, Esquire,* and *Men's*

Wear. Chain Store Age with its various editions and *Progressive Grocer, Hardware Retailer,* and *Footwear News* are trade magazines which provide valuable information for beginning retail merchants in those fields.

Offerings of Other Successful Stores. The offerings of other successful stores can aid beginning merchants in deciding what merchandise to carry in their stores. This source of information is particularly useful to smaller merchants who cannot afford some of the other more costly methods of finding out what target customers want. This method requires simply that local stores be visited, and that their offerings, price ranges, and customer responses to them be studied. A knowledge of what other successful stores are stocking and promoting can be useful not only to the beginning merchant who plans to sell similar merchandise but also to the merchant who plans to feature unique items. Ascertaining what other similar stores are selling can be beneficial to the merchant who plans to sell merchandise similar to or dissimilar from competition.

Controlling the Stock

The beginning retail merchant must have an adequate quantity of merchandise in stock to meet the requirements of the target market. If the merchandise inventory is inadequate, sales and profits will be lost. On the other hand, if the amount of stock is excessive relative to consumer demand, funds will be tied up in stock which is not selling, and this will adversely affect sales and profits. Thus, the principal purpose of stock control is to maintain a "good" assortment of stock which is in line with the store's sales.

Good stock control requires that the beginning merchant have correct, current, and all pertinent information. To provide such information, a merchant needs to set up controls on both a dollar and unit basis. Dollar control is exercised in terms of the amount of money, at retail prices, the merchant invests in the stock. Unit control is concerned with the individual items or pieces of merchandise which comprise the merchandise inventory. Dollar control attempts to answer the question of *how much money is in the budget* to invest in the merchandise inventory, while unit control goes further and attempts to answer the question of *what* is in the inventory to be controlled.

Set Up Classifications for Stock

To help control stock, classifications should be set up. Classification control refers to subdividing merchandise into rather narrow groups and then establishing a set of control records for each of the subgroups. Each class should represent a group of related merchandise. The merchandise may be grouped according to the department in which it is sold, by product category, or on a brand-model-price basis. A stock classification system enables the merchant to quickly spot voids where additional items are needed to meet demand and to identify areas where there may be excessive duplication of items in stock.

Merchandise in a department may be classified according to the needs and wants of shoppers. As such, merchandise classifications are set up on the basis of how customers shop. A merchandise classification for slacks is illustrated below.

Merchandise Classifications

Level 1 Classification	Level 2 Classification	Level 3 Classification	Level 4 Classification
boys' slacks	dress	pleated-front	slim sizes
his 'n hers	western	plain-front	husky sizes
men's	casual	beltless	regular sizes
women's	safari	belt-loop	extra tall

As shown in the table, a store may use several levels of merchandise classifications. The number of levels a merchant decides to establish

depends on the extent of control needed for the successful perfor-
mance of a department and the number of merchandise break-
downs that are necessary to provide a balanced assortment of goods.

Even if a store is not set up on a departmental basis, a classification control system still may be used. A women's wear merchant
may know that 15 to 16 percent of the store's annual sales are made
during the month of December. But the sales rate of individual
items will vary by merchandise classes. If a reasonable balance is to
be maintained between the stock and sales, information is needed
by individual lines. Dollar control on a classification basis can
provide an answer; it may, for example, reveal that 20 percent of the
leather goods sales volume is made in December because certain
leather items are much more commonly purchased as gifts than are
shoes and dresses.

Unit Control

As previously mentioned, unit control relates to individual or
pieces of items in the inventory. The beginning merchant can use a
unit control system to help make sure that there is an adequate
amount of depth in the assortment to meet the buying patterns of
the target customer. The nature of unit control can be further
clarified by reviewing some of the purposes it serves.

1. Unit control can be useful in facilitating the reordering of
merchandise so the merchant can maintain a good balance between
stocks and sales.

2. Unit records may be developed to follow the *age condition*
of the stock according to brands, prices, sizes, and models. This
would readily identify the slow-selling items.

3. A good unit system reveals what items are the most popular
sellers and those which are not as popular. This permits the merchant to concentrate on the brands, sizes, colors, and models that

require the least amount of effort to sell, so that stock-outs are reduced to a minimum.

4. Unit control can help identify to what extent the different vendors' lines are selling. In such case, the merchant may wish to maintain records on purchases, sales, markups, and markdowns by vendors.

5. Unit control may serve as a guide for sales promotion. Unit records can be used to facilitate the timing of promotions, and to show how the various items in the inventory respond to the promotional effort.

Dollar Control

A dollar control system requires that records be kept to provide data in terms of retail prices, which can be used as a guide in buying for the store. Dollar control can apply to the store as a whole, to departments, to classifications, or to price lines. As a financial control device, dollar control shows the investment pattern in the merchandise the store carries.

When dollar control is exercised on a departmental basis, sales, returns by customers, purchases, returns to vendors, markups, and stock turnovers should be maintained on a departmental basis. If a classification control system is used, the beginning merchant would need to maintain the records by types of merchandise carried within the department. For example, in the case of a beginning sporting goods merchant, data should be recorded separately for hunting equipment and supplies, fishing equipment and supplies, tennis equipment and supplies, and the like. Similarly, dollar control could be exercised on a price line basis within a department.

Under the dollar control system, the merchant may wish to maintain the inventory on a cost basis. This would require that the physical inventory figures be recorded at cost; purchases during the period are recorded at cost prices, which are available from pur-chase records or invoices furnished by suppliers; each sales trans-action is also recorded at cost prices. The book inventory at the cost figure may be used in situations where the merchandise carries a very high unit value, where there is a small number of transactions, and where there is a limited number of items carried in stock, as is usually the case for an appliance dealer. A major advantage of the cost method of keeping the books is that sales at the retail prices can be compared to the cost of goods sold on a daily basis. The dif-ference between the sales and cost of goods sold is the gross profit, which would also be available on a daily basis.

Visual Control

The simplest type of unit control is called *visual* or *mental* control. This is a method of checking the stock which is especially suited to the smaller retail merchant. This type of control exists when the merchant is physically close enough to the merchandise to actually see the changes occurring between the stock on hand and the sales rate. Visual control usually works well when (1) the items are of low unit value, (2) the items are continuously carried in stock, (3) the sales rate of the items is fairly stable from week to week, (4) there is considerable depth, (5) the needed stock can be quickly obtained from suppliers, and (6) the items are stored sepa-rately from other items in bins or shelf facings.

Never-Out Stock Lists

Every beginning retail merchant will sell some items on which an *out* condition will cause adverse customer reaction. To prevent or minimize stock-outs, the merchant may wish to maintain a *never-out* stock list. In the never-out system, a minimum quantity that should be on hand is assigned to each item, and the merchant may wish to set a maximum. The minimum should provide the merchant with a sufficient cushion to allow for time to replenish the brand before the out condition is reached. The never-out stock list is especially suited for staples that a store carries throughout the year or season, and that are reordered frequently.

In preparing the never-out stock list, the merchant needs to estimate (1) the weekly sales of each item on the list, (2) how long it takes to get delivery, (3) the frequency of reordering, and (4) what quantity of each to have on reserve to meet unusual demand situations. To illustrate, each week the retail merchant sells ten units of a never-out brand; delivery time is two weeks (from the time a reorder is placed with a supplier to readying the brand for sale); reorders are placed every four weeks; and twenty items are planned for reserve stock. The minimum is calculated as follows: multiply the delivery time in weeks by the weekly rate of sale and add the reserve stock ($2 \times 10 + 20 = 40$). The merchant would normally order four weeks' supply, or 40 units. Hence, the maximum commitment to this brand is 80 units. If a spot check on the brand reveals that 30 units are on hand rather than the planned 40, then the merchant should reorder 50 units, not the usual 40. The specific unit of control may be in terms of boxes or some other multiple units.

In the case of fashion goods which are not reordered on a regular basis, the above procedure does not apply. For fashion merchandise, the retail merchant needs sales information by style number, and often by size and color, on a daily basis. This information may be obtained from (1) duplicate sales checks, (2) stubs on price tickets, or (3) cash register tapes. The merchant can monitor the sale rate of each style by using one of the above three as the source. The book inventory figure by style at the end of any day can be calculated by subtracting the net sales from the previous day's inventory plus the amount of the purchases, if any, received into stock during the day. For example, at the beginning of the day on March 1 there are 10 units of Brand X in the inventory. If 5 units were sold during the day, and if 12 were received into stock during the day, the balance of Brand X in stock at the close of business on March 1 should be 17 ($10 + 12 - 5$).

Perpetual Stock Control

If a merchant wants to know the value of the merchandise inventory without taking a physical count of the stock on hand, records must be maintained for all merchandise acquisitions and all the merchandise that is sold. This requires the use of what is called a *perpetual stock control* system, which makes possible a record of stock balances on hand at any time the information is desired. When the perpetual stock control system is used, sales, merchandise receipts, adjustments for customers' returns, and returns to vendors should be posted as they occur. With these data, the stock on hand at any time is determined by adding the net purchases (gross purchases less purchases returned to vendors) to the beginning of period inventory and then subtracting sales for the period. To illustrate, assume the following hypothetical data:

Day	On Hand	Received	Sales
7/1	100		25
7/2	75		20
7/3	55	100	25
7/4	130		60
7/5	70		

All receipts and sales are posted on a daily basis and from this the number of units on hand is derived. If the book figures are accurately maintained, the book inventory balance should be the same as the number of units actually in stock. Any shortages are revealed when a complete physical inventory is taken, and if any discrepancies are disclosed the book inventory should be corrected at that time.

The perpetual inventory system is especially suited for a store selling items with large unit values, such as household furniture and appliances and apparels. It is also practical for commodities which are sold by the barrel or ton.

Periodic Stock Control

It is not always important for a retail merchant to know the exact balance of stock on hand at a given point in time, particularly if the store is selling numerous items which have a low unit value, such as nails carried in a hardware store. In this case, the merchant might elect to exercise stock control on a periodic basis, which requires that a physical count of the stock on hand be made to determine the amount of sales for the year. After the physical count is taken, this figure is then subtracted from the total purchases, at retail value, for the year. The result includes both sales and any retail reductions. After the retail reductions are determined and subtracted, a sales figure is derived. To illustrate, assume the following hypothetical data:

Retail purchases, July 1-June 30	$100,000
Inventory, at retail, June 30	40,000
Sales plus retail reductions, July 1-June 30	$ 60,000
Less: Retail reductions, July 1-June 30	5,000
Sales for the year	$ 55,000

Records of purchases and markdowns must be kept. Also, a record of all discounts granted to the store's employees or any special customers should be made. However, no record of each sale transaction is needed when the periodic stock control system is used, because sales for the year are a derived figure. The periodic stock control system is practical in cases where the merchant carries hundreds of relatively small, low-priced items, and where it is not cost effective for the merchant to maintain perpetual inventory records.

Planning the Stock

The merchandise inventory constitutes the largest single current asset of the store. Accordingly, stocks are among the most important items the merchant will want to plan. The planning of stock is required to adequately meet the needs of target customers and to avoid or minimize stock-out conditions. The proper planning of the inventories provides the basis for unit control and helps in determining the extent of depth and breadth in the assortment.

The planning of stock helps the merchant to maintain an inventory that is *balanced* in relation to anticipated sales. This means there must be adequate breadth in the assortment to meet the needs and wants of customers, and that the stock depth should conform with the rate of sales of each assortment factor such as size, color, and price range. Also, the inventory investment should be large enough to meet customer needs; at the same time, it should be small enough to realize a reasonable stock turn rate. In order to facilitate the planning of the necessary quantity of stock that should be on hand at the start of the month to meet customer needs, the merchant may use one of several methods. Two such methods, stock-sales ratios and weeks-of-supply, are covered in the following paragraphs.

Stock-Sales Ratios Method

Stock-sales ratios are useful and convenient planning guides that the beginning merchant may use in stock planning. They relate the stock as of a given date to the sales for the period (usually a month). For example, if the dollar value of the stock on hand January 1 is divided by sales for that month, it is called the January beginning-of-month (BOM) stock-sales ratio. To illustrate how the stock-sales ratio method is used, assume the beginning of period stock for a department is $18,000 at retail value, and the sales for the month are $9,000. The stock-sales ratio then would be 2.0. This means that if the estimated sales for the month are $20,000, and if the stock-sales ratio is 2.0, the value of the beginning-of-month stock is $40,000. This is the retail value of the stock that should be on hand at the beginning of the month to avoid stock-outs and to achieve a desired rate of stock turnover.

In planning BOM stock for a given month, the planner needs to know the BOM stock-sales ratio and the planned sales for the month. For example, if the BOM stock-sales ratio is 3.0, and the planned sales for the month are $10,000, then the planned BOM stock should be $30,000 (3.0 × $10,000). The BOM for each month of the planning period is calculated in a similar manner.

Stock-sales ratios may be calculated on a cost basis as well. Both the inventory and sales figures need to be converted to their cost equivalence if the ratio is to be correct. This can be done by simply multiplying the sales inventory at retail by the cost complement (100 percent minus the markup percent). For example, if sales are $50,000, the merchandise inventory at retail amounts to $150,000, and the average markup is 40 percent, then the cost of goods sold would be $30,000 [$50,000 × (100% − 40%)]; the cost value of the merchandise inventory would be $90,000 [$150,000 × (100% − 40%)]. In this case the stock-sales ratio would be 3.0 ($90,000/$30,000). The stock-sales ratios method is easy to apply in practice, and it is most advantageous for retail merchants who have highly variable or seasonal sales.

Weeks-of-Supply Method

A second method which the merchant can use to plan the beginning-of-month stock to obtain a desired rate of stock turnover is called weeks-of-supply method or number of weeks supply. Whenever this method is used, target figures in terms of a given number of weeks-of-supply must be established. If the annual planned stock turnover rate for a given department is 10, the stock on hand at any given time should be equal to approximately five weeks' supply (52 weeks ÷ 10 = 5.2). This means the amount of stock that should be on hand at the beginning of the month is approximately equal to the anticipated sales during the next five weeks. If the expected sales for the following five weeks amount to $20,000, and the rate of stock turnover is 10, the value of the stock that should be on hand at the beginning of the month would be

$200,000 ($20,000 × 10). The weeks-of-supply method is recommended for merchants whose sales are relatively stable throughout the year.

Rate of Stock Turnover

Selling stock converts the merchandise inventory into cash or, if the sales are made on credit, into receivables. The proceeds can be used to buy new stock which is then sold, and the process continues. The number of times the stock is sold refers to the rate of stock turnover. The concept of stock turnover is basic to an understanding of retail merchandising. It is a commonly used method to gauge the extent of balance between stocks and sales. It measures the rate at which stocks move into and out of the store or department. Also, the rate of stock turnover may be viewed as the number of times in a year (or a shorter time period) that the average inventory is sold and replenished.

Determining the Rate of Stock Turnover

The rate of stock turnover may be calculated either on a unit or dollar basis. If stocks are controlled on a unit basis, the retail merchant should also be interested in the rate of stock turnover by units. Knowing the unit turnover ratio serves as a guide to what quantities of the various brands or styles to carry. The following equation can be used to calculate the rate of turnover of stock on a unit basis:

$$\text{Rate of Stock Turnover} = \frac{\text{Number of units sold during the period}}{\text{Average number of units in stock during period}}$$

An appliance store merchant plans a turnover goal of 6.0 for the year. At the end of the year the records are checked, and it is determined that the merchant sold 75 appliance items during the year. The store had 16 units at the start of the year and 14 in stock at the end of the year. The average inventory would be 15 [(16 + 14) /2]. The rate of merchandise turnover in units would be 5.0 (75/15). This appliance merchant failed to reach the goal, which was 6.0, either because sales were not high enough or the average inventory was slightly too large. Thus, by either increasing sales by 15 units for the year, by reducing the average inventory to 12.5 units, or by increasing sales and reducing the average inventory by varying amounts, the desired rate of merchandise turnover could be attained.

Frequently a retail merchant will want to know the rate of stock turnover by departments, product lines, or brands. If this is the case, the inventory is not averaged for the store as a whole. Instead, the averaging of the inventory is done by departments, product lines, or brands. Breaking down the stock turnover ratios by departments or classifications facilitates stock analysis.

When the turnover rate of stock is calculated on a dollar basis, either cost or retail values are used, but it is not correct to mix the two in the same calculation. If merchants maintain their inventory records at cost, it is proper to calculate dollar turnover of merchandise at cost. In such a case, the cost of goods sold for the year is divided by the average inventory at cost. To illustrate: the cost of goods sold for the year is $45,000, and the average inventory at cost is $15,000. The dollar rate of stock turnover then is 3.0 ($45,000 divided by $15,000). In the case of those merchants who maintain their books at the retail value, the turnover rate is determined as follows:

$$\textbf{Rate of Stock Turnover, at retail } = \frac{\text{Net sales}}{\text{Average retail stock}}$$

To illustrate: assume that the dollar net sales are $100,000, and the average stock at retail is $25,000; the rate of stock turnover at retail would be 4.0 ($100,000/$25,000).

Calculation of Average Inventory

The value of the average inventory is obviously needed to calculate the unit or dollar stock turn ratio. But the average, whether in units or dollars, must be calculated. To ascertain the average inventory, simply sum up the values of the inventory which should be taken one or more times a year and divide the sum by the number of inventory counts. A merchant who takes a physical inventory only once a year, in January, would calculate average inventory by adding the inventory figure of the current year to the inventory figure of the preceding year, and then divide the sum by 2.0. For example, if the current inventory count is valued at $25,000, and the previous count was valued at $21,000, the average inventory would be $23,000—($25,000 plus $21,000)/2.0. A merchant who makes two inventory counts a year, one in January and one in July, would then sum up three inventory figures—the current January figure, the July inventory, and the previous January inventory—and divide by 3.0.

When the inventory figures used in calculating the average are abnormally low, this tends to yield a smaller average inventory. Consequently, the turnover ratio would be higher than otherwise. The beginning merchants are likely to conclude that they are realizing a higher rate of turnover than what might actually be the case. To get a more accurate picture of the average inventory and, thus, turnover ratio, a monthly inventory count should be used in calculating the average inventory. This would tend to smooth out the highs and lows in the inventory during the year.

Importance of a Relatively High Rate of Stock Turnover

If stock turns rapidly, the operating expense items related to owning and holding stock, particularly the inventory carrying costs, are reduced. When the investment in stock per dollar of sales is decreased, interest costs are reduced if the merchant uses outside financing; capital is more efficiently used if the merchant is self-financed. Second, a high turnover rate helps to ensure that fresh merchandise will be in stock. The morale of salespeople is likely to be higher when the stock is fresh and interesting than when it has been in the store for a long period of time. Third, a high turnover rate frees up capital funds which would be available for unexpected special buys. This is the consequence of funds being tied up in stock shorter periods of time. Fourth, the cost of inventory obsolescence will be reduced. If the stock is in the store for shorter periods, this tends to reduce the amount of inventory obsolescence. Fifth, with a high stock turn ratio, the gross profit margin should improve, because fewer markdowns will be needed to sell the merchandise. Sixth, since the investment in stock represents a merchant's largest single investment in current assets, a high rate of stock turnover will have a direct impact on the rate of asset turnover, i.e., the number of sales dollars generated to each dollar invested in assets will go up.

Finally, a comparatively high rate of stock turnover helps the merchant to make better use of *leverage*. Leverage refers to the extent to which outside sources of funds are used to finance the business. For example, when a retail merchant purchases merchandise under terms of net 30 days and is able to sell this merchandise in less than 30 days, the investment in that merchandise is being financed entirely by the supplier. Thus, the higher the turnover rate of stock, the smaller the amount of the merchant's own capital that would be needed to finance the merchandise inventory.

Ways to Improve the Rate of Stock Turnover

If the rate of stock turnover is relatively low, the merchant should attempt to improve it. Sometimes, however, this is "easier said than done," as slow-selling stock may suggest a lack of consumer taste for it. But with a carefully planned strategy, stock sales can be improved. This can be accomplished by (1) increasing sales with a less-than-proportionate increase in stock, or by (2) reducing the amount of stock on hand. Of course, the first of these two is more difficult to accomplish, all things being equal, because customers generally prefer to select from a broad assortment of merchandise. Thus, if the size of the assortment mix is reduced, customers may cut back on their purchases, because fewer options will exist. Also, to a large extent the ability of a retail merchant to increase sales is dependent upon the existing business conditions and the competitive environment, neither of which is under the control of the store. On the other hand, the amount of funds invested in merchandise is an internal matter which is controllable by the store proprietor. Accordingly, the amount of purchases can be cut back when conditions warrant it. Hence, it is easier to trim the size of the inventory than it is to get more sales from the same inventory size or the same sales from a smaller inventory.

Chapter Two

PLANNING THE CASH FLOW

Until funds begin to flow into the business on a regular basis, the beginning merchant must have adequate cash on hand to meet current obligations during the early months of operation. Among these obligations are salaries and wages, advertising and promotional expenses, taxes, and overhead expenses. The number of months of operating funds a beginning retail merchant needs to have on hand when the establishment opens for business ranges from one month to a year. As a minimum, the beginning merchant should have enough cash on hand when the business opens to cover operations for a three-month period, or enough to last until the merchandise inventory turns over at least once. This means that if the average inventory sells four times a year, a three month's supply of cash funds should be on hand when the merchant opens for business. Once the average inventory is sold, at least a portion of the receipts from it can be used to help cover current operating expenses.

The merchant who sells merchandise which turns over rapidly will need fewer months of cash at the start of the business than the merchant who sells merchandise that turns over more slowly. For example, when a grocer with a relatively high merchandise turn rate opens for business, fewer months of operating funds need to be on hand than what a jewelry merchant with a slower average merchandise turn rate would need to have on hand.

An adequate amount of operating funds is critically important for the beginning merchant. Current financial obligations must be met when they fall due. Creditors, employees, and overhead costs must be paid promptly. If the current obligations cannot be met, the store will soon be faced with a serious cash flow problem. Consequently, suppliers will become alarmed, and employees who are not paid promptly will suffer from a lack of morale. Thus, an inadequate amount of operating capital funds could result in bankruptcy for the business.

To prevent a cash crisis from developing early in the store's operation, cash flow needs of the store should be carefully planned and managed. One step that should be taken when such planning is being undertaken is to decide on what time period the plan is to cover. It is advisable to plan for a six-month or twelve-month period; once the cash needed is forecast, the planning period chosen can be broken down into months or weeks.

In planning the cash needs for the store, both the expected cash receipts and disbursements should be considered. The expected amount of net increase (or decrease) in cash receipts should be added to (or subtracted from) the beginning cash balance in order to determine what the expected cash balance will be at the end of the month or year.

Cash Receipts

A retail merchant's principal source of cash receipts will be the proceeds from the sale of merchandise. This being the case, the merchant will need to boost sales in order to increase the cash receipts. On the other hand, if sales decline during a particular period, cash receipts will correspondingly drop. Because of this, there will be variations in receipts from month to month, creating an irregular monthly cash flow.

If a merchant sells for cash only, or accepts bank cards, cash receipts and net sales for the period will be equal (except for the bank discount fee if bank cards are accepted). If sales are made on credit, creating an *accounts receivable* situation, the cash receipts and net sales for any one period will not necessarily be the same. The amount of cash received during the period will depend on what proportion of net sales is made on a cash basis and the rate at which collections are made on the credit customers' accounts.

Cash Sales. The small retail merchant may want to sell only for cash. It reduces paperwork and eliminates any possible uncollectable accounts. When sales are made on a cash basis only, cash receipts will equal the estimated sales for the planning period. Selling on a cash basis eliminates the need for paying a bank discount charge, and there are no accounts receivables to collect.

Collections on Accounts Receivable. If a retail merchant extends credit to customers, accounts receivable are created. Cash receipts are not realized until the receivables are collected. For this reason, the amount of the cash received during the period will not be the same as net sales. A lag will exist between sales and the ultimate receipt of cash from those sales. Hence, the cash received during a particular period will depend on the amount of cash sales *plus* the proportion of accounts receivable that are collectable during that period. Also, some cash received during the current period will be from sales made in a previous period.

Other Income. Sometimes merchants receive revenue from sources other than the sale of merchandise. For example, if a merchant has surplus cash invested in interest-bearing notes, the interest income would be considered *other income* because it was generated from a source other than the sale of merchandise.

Cash Disbursements

The retail merchant makes cash disbursements to meet current operating expenses and to pay for currently maturing liabilities or obligations. The amount to be paid out will vary during each period because some of the operating expenses are variable. Salaries and wages of employees constitute the largest proportion of a retail merchant's total operating expenses, but these vary from period to period, particularly if part-time salespeople are employed by the store and if there are any overtime hours. Rental expenses, however, are fixed during the normal operating cycle. The currently maturing obligations, such as notes payable, are stable, and disbursements for these can easily be predicted.

Cash Disbursements for Merchandise Purchased. When merchandise is bought for the store, an obligation is created to pay for it. The agreement may be to pay for the goods upon arrival or at a subsequent date, which would create an accounts payable account. In either case, an obligation to make a cash disbursement is created when the merchandise is purchased. By taking advantage of any cash discount which might be available, the amount to be paid is reduced by the amount of the discounts taken.

Cash Disbursements for Store Operating Expenses. A second type of cash disbursement is made to cover operating expenses. Included in this category are rent, taxes, salaries and wages, advertising and promotion, supplies, and overhead expenses, including heating, lighting, and telephone services. Most of these expenses will vary according to the season of the year and with sales volume. Because many of the operating expenses are variable, cash disbursements for them will also vary. Thus, the level of cash disbursements during a particular operating period depends upon the amount of accounts payable and other liabilities coming due and on the level of operating expenses incurred during the period.

Planning Fixed Capital Funds

Besides the planning of funds to meet current operations, the beginning retail merchant must also plan capital funds which are needed to acquire fixtures and equipment to be used by the store. These may include cash registers, counters, stock bins, carts, trucks, display tables, racks, etc. The capital funds required for these items can be determined by deciding on the type and quantity needed, securing prices, and adding them up. The total figure represents the amount of capital funds needed to acquire fixed assets.

Unlike the funds for current operations which are needed for periods ranging from 30 to 90 days, fixed capital funds are needed by retail merchants for substantially longer periods of time. Because of this, a different kind of loan is needed. In general, intermediate term credit, which is granted to retail merchants by banks for periods of one to ten years, is needed. This type of long-term credit is required to finance fixed assets which will depreciate over time. Essentially, a formal agreement would be entered into with a bank, and a line of credit is established to finance the purchase of store equipment and fixtures.

In some cases, the purchase of equipment and fixtures will not have to be made outright. The retail merchant may lease the needed capital equipment and fixtures. By leasing, the merchant would not need to borrow funds to buy capital equipment but would only need to pay a rental charge on it. Also, by leasing equipment, the merchant would need less long-term capital funds for the business.

Chapter Three

PLANNING THE
INTERIOR LAYOUT OF THE STORE

The interior layout of a retail store refers to the arrangement of equipment, fixtures, displays, aisles, and check-outs to have maximum impact on the customer. From an economic standpoint, all space in a store is scarce and exists in short supply. The merchant is required to pay rent on every gross square foot of space the store occupies. Because of this, it is critically important that layout helps to accomplish the goal of maximizing sales productivity.

Layout should facilitate the merchandising function by making the merchandise on display visually attractive to customers and by facilitating the shopping process. The layout arrangement used in the store should harmonize with the type of store. The fast food merchant, for example, will want a layout arrangement that will move large numbers of people into and out of the establishment fast, while the specialty store merchant will want a layout arrangement designed to encourage customers to spend more time in the store and shop.

Factors Affecting the Interior Layout Arrangement

The interior layout of a store is affected by numerous factors. The size of the store, the shape of the store, the type and quantity of merchandise sold, the type of selling method to be employed, the type of store fixtures to be used, and the customer traffic flow must all be carefully considered before deciding the interior layout arrangement.

Size of the Store. The total gross square feet of space a store occupies affects the type of layout arrangement a merchant can use. In a comparatively small store, the merchant will have aisles which are narrow and display shelves that are above eye level in order to stock more merchandise. There will be less "openness" in smaller stores as compared to larger ones. In the larger stores there exists a greater opportunity for openness in the type of layout arrangement a merchant can use. The aisles may be wide and the display shelves maintained at eye level. The merchants with large stores have more opportunity for variation in the type of layout arrangement used than those who have small stores.

The Shape of the Store. The physical shape (square, rectangular, circular, or U-shaped) of the store affects the manner in which space is allocated to the various selling and non-selling departments. The location of permanent equipment, such as air-conditioning units, doors for receiving new merchandise, and customer entrances will also affect the interior layout arrangement of the store. In addition, the shape of the store will influence the types of fixtures that can be effectively used in the store.

Type and Quantity of Merchandise Sold. The layout arrangement used by a merchant is greatly influenced by the type and quantity of merchandise stocked. A household furniture merchant needs a considerable amount of open space to display the furniture, while a jewelry merchant needs relatively little space but a considerable amount of store security. In the case of stores using self-service selling, such as a variety store, a good deal of openness is needed in the layout arrangement. Items which are sold in large quantities would require more space and may be located near the storeroom to facilitate restocking the displays.

Type of Selling Method to Be Employed. The type of selling method used by the retail merchant affects the layout arrangement that will be used. When the *self-service* method of selling is employed, the merchandise is displayed and arranged so that customers can make their selections without any assistance from salespeople. Open display shelves and tables are typically used, with some merchandise being placed on racks and "islands" arranged conveniently for the customers. With self-service selling, the traditional *grid* method of arranging the shelves, tables, and racks is used. The grid arrangement utilizes floor space most economically by having the maximum amount of merchandise per square foot of selling space on display.

When the merchandise sold requires fitting, as in some items of clothing, or when greater store security is necessary, as for expensive jewelry, the *saloon* method of selling may be used. In saloon selling customers are seated while being shown the merchandise by salespeople. Much of the merchandise sold on this basis is displayed and arranged to minimize customer accessibility to it and to minimize potential shoplifting. Merchandise is contained either in locked glass cases, behind the counter beyond the reach of the customer, or in a reserve stockroom near the selling floor.

Type of Store Fixtures to Be Used. Another factor to be considered by the retail merchant with respect to layout is the type of fixtures to be used. Today, store fixtures are more flexible and adjustable than in the past. They have interchangeable parts and can be used in different areas within the store. This kind of flexibility gives the merchant more options in layout arrangements, and it permits the merchant to easily adjust to the seasons of the year, the volume of sales being handled, and the buying habits of customers. The lighter, more flexible fixture designs allow a merchant to completely rearrange the interior layout in a very short period of time when conditions warrant this.

Customer Traffic Flow. The layout of the store should be such that customers can get to all parts of the selling area with a minimum of inconveniences. The main aisles should be wider and designed to accommodate a substantially greater volume of store traffic than secondary aisles.

The arrangement of the interior of the store can be effective in directing the flow of customers. The grid layout arrangement can be used to steer store traffic in a predetermined manner. Items should be arranged in the store to get a maximum amount of exposure to store traffic. Items which are strong traffic builders, such as meat in a food store and suits in an apparel store, should be placed where they will "pull" traffic past the weak traffic-building items.

Space Allocation Methods

The sales potential of a department is an important factor in allocating space to merchandise in a store. This means the greater the sales potential of a given department, the greater the amount of space that the merchant should allocate to it. A grocery store would not give its skimmed milk as much space as whole milk in the dairy case, since skimmed milk sales would normally be considerably less. Furthermore, allocating more space to skimmed milk is not likely to increase its sales significantly.

Other factors may impact on space allocation. There are certain kinds of goods which, by their nature, simply need more space than others in a store. Appliances require a good deal of space; household furnishings need a lot of space; and during the Christmas season, toys require more space than most other departments in a store. At the other extreme, costume jewelry requires a comparatively small amount of space even though its sales productivity is usually quite high. If a department is dominant in establishing the image or reputation of a store, such as women's dresses, coats, and sportswear in an apparel store, it might be allocated more display space than other departments in the store.

Space-Productivity Ratios. This is one method which

might be used to allocate space to a department in a store. Space-productivity ratios refer to the dollar sales each square foot of space in a store generates for the merchant. In using this method, the planned sales of a proposed department are divided by the sales per square foot of selling space allocated to comparable departments of other stores to determine the amount of space to be allocated to the proposed department. When this method of allocating space is used, the merchant needs to know (1) the expected sales volume for the entire store, (2) the proportion of the total store sales each selling department is expected to generate, and (3) the sales per square foot of selling space of comparable stores.*

The space-productivity ratio method for determining departmental space requirements is computed as follows. Assume a new specialty store is proposed, with projected sales the first year of $100,000, and with departmental sales as a percent of total sales as below:

1. Shoes, 60 percent.
2. Hats, 25 percent.
3. Leather goods, 15 percent.

Assume further that the typical specialty store's sales per square foot of selling space is $128.83. Now, the amount of space to be allocated to these departments in the new store can be calculated using the following procedure:

1. For each department, multiply the total store planned sales by each of their percentage shares. The results are as follows:

a. Shoes, $60,000 ($100,000 × 60%).
b. Hats, $25,000 ($100,000 × 25%).
c. Leather goods, $15,000 ($100,000 × 15%).

The above are the amounts of sales that each of the departments should generate.

---

*Sales per square foot of selling space are published by the National Retail Merchants Association in its "Financial and Operating Results of Department and Specialty Stores."

2. By using $128.83, which is the typical specialty store's sales per square foot of selling space, the amount of space to allocate to each department can be calculated as follows:

a. **Shoe department**

$$\frac{\$60,000 \text{ (planned sales for the shoe department)}}{\$128.83 \text{ (the sales per square foot of selling space allotted to typical specialty stores)}}$$

This ratio yields 465.7, which is the number of square feet of space that should be allocated to the shoe department.

b. **Hat department**

$$\frac{\$25,000}{\$128.83} = 194.1$$

c. **Leather goods department**

$$\frac{\$15,000}{\$128.83} = 116.4$$

The results are that approximately 466, 194, and 116 square feet of selling space will be allocated to the shoe, hat, and leather goods departments, respectively. This is a rough approximation of the amount of space that would be allocated; it does not guarantee optimum results, as the figures are advisory.

The use of space-productivity ratios as a basis for allocating space in the store to departments tend to vary by the type of establishment. In the case of wearing apparel and general merchandise stores, sales per square foot of space is the typical criterion used; in food stores, variety stores, and hardware stores, the amount of linear shelf space is the standard used; and for frozen food items, the cubic feet of freezer space could be used.

The Model Stock Procedure. A model stock is an optimal stock in terms of styles, price lines, sizes, colors, and materials that customers want. For the beginning merchant, there is no past experience to serve as a basis for model stock planning. However, helpful information can be obtained by ascertaining what stocks are carried by other prosperous merchants featuring the same line of merchandise, or by consulting key suppliers. The use of the model stock concept as a basis for allocating space in a store involves the following steps.

1. On the basis of standards established by similar type and size of stores, the proper balance between stocks and sales can be established. For example, if the operating data of other similar stores reveal that $3 of inventory at retail prices is necessary to generate $1 of sales by a store, the stock-sales ratio would be 3 to 1.

2. On the basis of stock-sales ratios established by similar stores, the merchant can determine the amount of space required to accommodate a given assortment of merchandise, or a department. Experience in the supermarket field might show that a stock-sales ratio of 3 to 1 is required for canned soup. Assume that sales of this item in the average supermarket amount to 400 units a week, and that the retail price per unit is $0.30. The dollar sales of soup would be $120 a week (400 × $0.30). With the established stock-sales ratio of 3 to 1, $360 in the soup inventory is required for the week, or 1,200 cans ($360/$0.30). If one linear foot of shelf space will house 12 cans of this size soup, then 1,200 cans will require 100 linear feet of shelf space. A similar procedure could be used to allocate space to other items carried. If the total of the calculated space needed according to this procedure is greater than the space actually available in the store, then all or some of the departmental allocations should be revised, perhaps on a proportionate basis.

Of course some space in a store is needed for non-selling activities. This non-selling space tends to increase with the size of the store. In a small store, a major proportion of the non-selling activities, such as checking, inspecting, and marking the merchandise, may be conducted by employees on the sales floor. The non-selling area for the small merchant may comprise a desk or small office for the owner/manager, a washroom, space for receiving merchandise, and some storage space for reserve stock.

Planning the Location of Stock Within the Store

The types of goods being sold influences where they should be placed in the store. Impulse items which customers do not make a special trip to buy should be located where they will get maximum exposure to store traffic. Thus, impulse items should be placed up front, or along the main aisles where most shoppers pass by.

Some merchandise, such as those items (called *shopping goods*) which customers usually compare on the basis of price, quality, and style before purchasing, has strong traffic-generating or pulling power. This type of merchandise should be placed in the less accessible areas of the store to pull customers past other merchandise which does not generate its own store traffic. Convenience goods and accessories are moderate traffic builders and should be made relatively accessible to store traffic. The merchant might wish to place these near the front of the store and along the main aisles.

Household furniture and appliances which customers buy only after deliberating for some time, should be located away from the high-traffic areas in the store. If the store occupies only one level, these items should be placed in the rear; if it occupies several levels, they should go on the upper levels. The object is to minimize possible traffic congestion in the more heavily traveled areas of the store. Since household furniture and appliance shoppers take their time deliberating, locating these items out of the high-traffic areas in the store helps to reduce possible congestion.

Goods which are used together or which complement one another might be placed in the same general area, since customers tend to buy related merchandise on the same shopping trip. Films, flash bulbs, and other camera accessories should be placed near the cameras. The placing of similar merchandise in the same general area usually results in additional sales being made by the store which may not otherwise by realized. Seasonal items, like impulse items, should be placed right up front so they can get a maximum amount of exposure to store traffic. Finally, the least valuable space in the store, that which has the least amount of store traffic, should be used for non-selling activities.

Chapter Four

PLANNING THE PRICING STRATEGY

The pricing decisions the beginning retail merchant makes are critically important to the success of the store. Prices influence the type of customers who will be attracted to a store. Prices also affect a store's sales revenue, profit margins, and image.

To facilitate pricing decisions, the merchant might want to develop a price policy for the store which would serve as an overall guide in pricing situations. Price policy sets general principles or rules the merchant should follow in making routine pricing decisions. Examples of price policies a merchant might adopt are as follows:

1. To never be undersold by competitors.

2. To sell at prices above competitors' in order to appeal to a "prestige" market.

3. To attempt to build a large volume of store traffic.

4. To price in order to provide the store with a given percentage return on its investment in the inventory.

5. To price in order to realize a given percentage of net profit to sales.

In developing pricing strategies, the merchant should be cognizant of the role price plays in the eyes of the target customers. Price appeals are frequently the key variable which attract the target customer. On one hand, some customers are willing to pay a comparatively high price because of the expectation of getting a higher quality product, or because of the prestige usually associated with higher priced stores. But many customers are highly sensitive to price differences among merchants and tend to shun those whose prices are perceived as being high. Hence, one merchant might be successful with a high price, while another can be equally effective by using a relatively low pricing strategy. The two types of stores are appealing to different market segments. When setting price policy, a retail merchant has the option of pricing *at the market,* pricing *above the market,* or pricing *below the market.*

When a retail merchant prices at the market, the objective is to match the prices of direct competitors who handle comparable merchandise. This approach to pricing is appropriate when the store has no particular advantage over competitors as far as location, service offerings, product quality, and assortment are concerned. Other reasons a retail merchant might price at the market are customer expectations, a desire to avoid a price war with competitors, and uncertainty with respect to what the demand might be for the merchandise or services sold.

To set prices higher than those of direct competitors, the retail merchant must be able to clearly differentiate the store from competitors', so that customers will be attracted to the store in spite of the higher prices. The differentiation can be based on such factors as location of the store, customer services, product quality, assortment, and the general reputation or image of the store. A merchant might decide to price above the market if the store's operating costs are higher than competitors', if a prestige reputation is desired, if the products sold are superior to those offered by competitors, or if the merchant wishes to operate on a high-margin, low-volume basis.

Some merchants who assign a very important role to pricing may attempt to set prices which are lower than those charged by competitors. Pricing below the market is very popular today as illustrated by the pervasiveness of discounting. This is not advisable to a merchant unless the store is able to earn a satisfactory profit margin on the low-margin merchandise with a higher sales volume. A retail merchant may price below the market if the operating costs are lower than competitors' or if the products carried are lower in quality than those of competitors. Also, a merchant may price below the market if the store's policy is one of high volume and low margin per unit sold.

Planning Markups

In the process of making a product or service available to the public, merchants incur several different kinds of expenses, ranging from salaries and wages to rent and promotional costs. In addition, the merchant desires to earn a profit on the investment in the business. To cover the cost of operating the business and to earn a profit margin, the merchant will want to set a retail selling price on the merchandise and services sold above their costs to the store. Markups are generally used by merchants to cover operating expenses and to provide a profit margin for the store.

Markup refers to the amount which is added to the cost of the offering to arrive at the selling, or retail, price. It may be expressed in terms of dollars or as a percentage. An item which costs $8 and sells for $12 carries a markup of $4, or 33⅓ percent, based on the retail price. The concept of markup may be used to cover a single item, as in the preceding example, or it may be used to cover all of the items in an entire line or department. In the latter case, all dress shoes in a shoe department may carry a 50 percent markup.

Vendors' Suggested Retail Prices

Some suppliers recommend prices at which retail merchants are expected to sell the merchandise. When this is the case, the suggested retail price is assumed to be high enough to permit the merchant to earn a reasonable profit margin on the merchandise sold. But for competitive reasons merchants who carry such merchandise are frequently forced to sell it at prices below those suggested by suppliers. The vendors' suggested retail prices are only advisory for the merchant. Since resale price maintenance laws have been abolished, suppliers cannot legally hold merchants to the vendors' suggested retail prices.

Markup Percentages

Before an item or a line of merchandise is placed on display in the store, the retail merchant needs to decide what initial markup percentage to apply. The appropriate markup percentage is calculated to cover operating expenses and earn a profit. The amount of the markup percent is based on several factors, including the operating expenses, the desired profit, and the anticipated retail reductions (markdowns, employee discounts, and shortages). The equation that is used to ascertain the initial markup percent is as follows:

Initial markup% =
$$\frac{\% \text{ Operating expenses } + \% \text{ Net profit } + \% \text{ Reductions}}{\% \text{ Net sales } + \% \text{ Reductions}}$$

The operating expenses, net profit desired before taxes, and reductions are all based on net sales (the 100 percent amount). Because of this, the markup percentage to be determined by the preceding equation is based on retail prices and not on the cost of the merchandise. To illustrate, assume that on a given line of merchandise a merchant's operating expenses amount to 25 percent of net sales; net profit before taxes, 12 percent; and retail reductions, 4 percent. Then, the initial markup for a merchant with these figures should be 39.4 percent by substituting these figures in the preceding equation.

$$\text{Initial markup \%} = \frac{25\% + 12\% + 4\%}{100\% + 4\%}$$

$$= \frac{41\%}{104\%}$$

$$= 0.394 \text{ or } 39.4\%$$

What this means for the merchant using these figures is that a markup of 39.4 percent on the retail price is needed to arrive at the desired price. If a line of refrigerators costs an appliance dealer $300 each, and if they are marked up 39.4 percent of the retail base, the unit retail price is determined as follows:

$$\textbf{Retail price} = \frac{\$ \text{ Cost}}{100\% - \% \text{ markup}}$$

Substituting in the equation,

$$\begin{aligned}\text{Retail price} \\ \text{(a unit)}\end{aligned} = \frac{\$300}{100\% - 39.4\%}$$

$$= \frac{\$300}{60.6\%}$$

$$= \$495.05$$

This means that if the merchant's operating expenses were 25 percent of net sales; retail reductions, 4 percent; and the items sell for $300 each, the net profit before taxes should be $59.41 ($495.05 x 12%). The net profit of 12 percent was accounted for in the initial markup on the refrigerators.

It is advisable that the markup percent be based on the retail price, since it is customary to express the operating expenses as a percent of net sales. A merchant may wish, however, to know what the markup percent is when it is expressed in terms of both retail and cost. It should be noted that when the markup is based on the retail price, it is always a smaller percentage amount than when it is based on cost. A 50 percent markup based on the retail price is the same as a 100 percent markup based on the cost price. The markup percent based on the retail price is calculated by using the following equation:

$$\textbf{Markup \% on retail} = \frac{\text{Retail} - \text{Cost}}{\text{Retail}}$$

A merchant buys 200 umbrellas for \$1,400 and retails them for \$2,100 or \$10.50 each. By applying the preceding equation, the markup percent on retail becomes

$$\frac{\$2,100 - \$1,400}{\$2,100} = \frac{\$700}{\$2,100}$$

$$= 0.333 \text{ pr } 33.3\%$$

Thus, the merchant's markup was 33.3 percent.

If the merchant desires to know what the markup percent is on a cost base, the following equation applies:

$$\textbf{Markup \% on cost} = \frac{\text{Retail} - \text{Cost}}{\text{Cost}}$$

Using the same facts presented in the preceding illustration, the markup percent on a cost base is 50 percent, calculated as follows:

$$\text{Markup \% on cost} = \frac{\$2,100 - \$1,400}{\$1,400}$$

$$= \frac{\$700}{\$1,400}$$

$$= 0.50 \text{ or } 50\%$$

Thus, a 33⅓ percent markup on a retail price base is the same as a 50 percent markup on a cost base. When the dollar markup is stated as a percent of cost, it is usually easier to apply than the equivalent markup percent on the retail base. For example, a 50 percent markup on retail is the same as a 100 percent markup based on cost (sometimes called a *keystone* markup), which means that the retail price is arrived at simply by doubling the cost of the merchandise to the store.

Planning Markdowns

A markdown is a form of price adjustment which negatively affects profit margins because it is a *reduction* in the original or previous selling price of merchandise. It is a means by which the retail merchant can adjust the retail price of merchandise to conform with demand. A supermarket merchant may decide to reduce the price of bananas on Saturday afternoon to avoid the risk of carrying this perishable item in stock over the weekend. Near the end of a season, a specialty merchant may decide to take drastic price reductions on a line of coats to clear out this stock which is no longer acceptable to consumers at the original selling price. A merchant may decide to lower the price on a line of merchandise showing no depreciation in value in order to attract store traffic and stimulate sales of other merchandise throughout the store. If some of this merchandise remains unsold at the end of the sale, it can be remarked at the original retail price and returned to the regular stock. A markdown can serve as a sales promotion device, as a means of meeting competition, or to turn over slow-selling stock.

When it is determined that stock will not sell at the initial retail price, it is advisable to reduce the price even if some gross margin is lost. The longer the merchandise is in stock, the less likely it will sell at the initial retail price. Some markdowns are unavoidable, regardless of how carefully a merchant has selected the items. Market conditions change, and customers' buying habits and tastes also change over time. These factors also affect the saleability of merchandise.

Similar to markups, markdowns may be expressed in percentage terms. The dollar markdown may be expressed as a percentage of the original retail price or as a percentage of the actual selling price. To illustrate, assume an item had an original retail price of $50 and is marked down to \$40 and sold. The markdown percentage is calculated as follows:

$$\textbf{Markdown \%} \quad = \quad \frac{\text{Original retail} \; - \; \text{Actual retail}}{\text{Actual retail}}$$

Substituting in the equation,

$$\text{Markdown \%} \quad = \quad \frac{\$50 \; - \; \$40}{\$40} = \frac{\$10}{\$40} = 0.25 \text{ or } 25\%$$

If this markdown is expressed as a percentage of the original retail price, it would be 20 percent (\$10/\$50), the dollar markdown divided by the original retail price. When this dollar markdown is based on the original retail price, it can be referred to as *20% off* the original price. A merchant could promote this size markdown either as a *25% price reduction* or as a *20% off original price* sale.

The timing of the markdown can be critical for a merchant. If a markdown is taken too soon in the season, the store loses some of its potential sales revenue due to the price cut. If a markdown is taken too late in the season, the store may also lose some potential profit margin if some of the merchandise does not sell at all. Markdowns should be taken when the season's end approaches, when wholesale prices decline on the line, or when suppliers begin to place comparable or substitute items on the market. In this latter case, suppliers will generally encourage retail merchants to take markdowns on the old stock and sell it prior to the introduction of the new line.

In general, the first markdown taken on an item is the least expensive price reduction the merchant takes. When the first markdown is taken on a line of merchandise, it should be sufficient to move a significant proportion of it. If additional markdowns are warranted to sell the goods, they become increasingly more expensive to the merchant due to the increased costs of handling the merchandise and depreciation or obsolescence. These additional expenses tend to cut further into the store's profit margin.

If markdowns do not move the goods and the stock is carried over to the next season, as in the case of winter clothing, it becomes even more costly to the merchant. Frequently the price must be reduced the following season because the goods may no longer be fashion current. When seasonal merchandise is carried over to the next season, it reduces the merchandise turn rate and adversely affects the merchants' profit margin.

Planning What Price Lines to Carry

As a part of the merchandise assortment planning, the retail merchant needs to decide on the number of price lines, or points, to feature in the assortment, especially in the case of apparels. In using the price lining concept, it is customary that buying for the store be concentrated around three key price points for each line of merchandise. The sale of a line of dresses in a popular dress shop may concentrate around the following prices: $18, $25, and $35. The shop may also feature some supplementary price lines, selling at prices within or perhaps outside the range indicated here. Some supplementary lines may retail at $14.99, $21.95, and $29.95. But the major merchandising effort may be concentrated on the $18, $25, and $35 price lines if they prove to be the best selling lines. If these price lines prove to be satisfactory, the sales-volume distribution may concentrate around them:

$18 price line	33%
$25 price line	46%
$35 price line	21%
	100%

The percentages indicate consumer preferences for the various price lines. The inventory distribution by price line should follow the sales pattern of the lines. Whenever a shift occurs in the percent of sales distribution by price points, this would indicate what change is taking place in buyer preference for each price line. If customers do not perceive the price points as being fair given the quality, the price points may have to be changed or the quality upgraded.

The price line structure for a class of merchandise may change from one season to another. During the spring and summer season an apparel store may carry more lightweight or washable clothing at several price points below those of fall and winter merchandise.

There are some advantages of price lining from the standpoint of the retail merchant. Possible confusion by consumers is reduced when the merchandise assortments are restricted to a few price points in a line. If there are only a few price points, salespeople can become better acquainted with them and are likely to make fewer mistakes. Selling is facilitated, and customer goodwill is enhanced. By restricting the number of price lines, the merchant's investment in inventory will be smaller; merchandise turnover should increase; markdowns should decrease; and the cost of storage is reduced. Also, buying for the store is simplified, because store buyers can concentrate on items which will fit the predetermined price lines.

Leader and Promotional Pricing

As mentioned, the principal reason for price reductions is the expectation of increasing sales on the items offered at the lower margins. However, the retail merchant may take a very low markup for the purpose of generating store traffic and selling other merchandise at the regular markup prices. When items are intentionally sold at low markup prices for the purpose of drawing customers to the store, it is referred to as *leader* pricing. A few items from different departments may be selected as leaders, but a merchant may want to use an entire department, such as a shoe department in a department store, as leader. In either case, the reasoning behind leader pricing is that the leaders will generate a large number of customers who will also buy enough of the non-leader items at the regular markup prices to at least compensate for the price reductions taken on the leader items.

Items which are good candidates as leaders are likely to have certain characteristics. First, they should be items that are used by a broad spectrum of people and that are purchased somewhat frequently. Milk and soft drinks in a supermarket would be good candidates as leaders. Second, the items should have a well-known price so that shoppers will know they are getting a bargain. The third characteristic of a leader is that it should be a *small-ticket* item. For example, the item may be selling for less than $1 in a food store and less than $5 in a discount or variety store to qualify.

A merchant's policy with respect to promotions and special sales tends to influence price adjustments on some merchandise. Similar to leader pricing, promotional pricing is expected to attract people to the store who may not have otherwise come. The objective of promotional pricing is twofold: (1) that customers will not only buy the sale item but regular merchandise as well, and (2) that customers can be induced to trade up to a higher priced item from the low priced sale item. In order to accomplish this goal, the specific items which are selected as promotionals carry a lower than usual markup.

When the merchant's sales are sluggish, some merchandise may be bought especially for promotional purposes, designed to build store traffic and to generate enthusiasm among the salespeople. Promotionals may be run seasonally, such as New Year's sale, Easter sale, or pre-Fourth of July sale, or they may be run on a weekly or monthly basis, depending on the store's objectives and on what image the merchant wants to project.

Price Endings, Even-Odd Usages

In setting the retail price on a product a retail merchant usually has the option of either increasing or reducing the markup price by a few cents. A merchant may adopt a policy of using prices which end in zero, nine, or five. For example, the price of a ballpoint pen may be set at 99¢, 95¢, or $1. A merchant may opt for either 99¢ or 95¢ on the grounds that customers will buy a larger quantity of the pens at one of the odd prices, or that the odd price ending represents a bargain to the shopper.

The higher the price of the merchandise, the greater the tendency for retail merchants to use zero price endings, particularly if the merchant wants to establish a quality image. For example, a suit may be marked at $150 rather than $149.99. At this price range, an odd price ending would not be nearly as noticeable in the eyes of shoppers as would be an odd price ending for items selling in the $1 range.

Chapter Five

PLANNING THE ADVERTISING AND PROMOTIONAL STRATEGY

After a retail merchant stocks and opens the store for business, customers do not automatically beat a path to the doors. Potential customers must be informed that a new retail operation exists. They must be told what merchandise and services are offered. Customers must first be attracted to the store and then persuaded to buy once they come in. Then merchants must continually remind customers about their store and about any changes that are taking place in the product or service offerings. This important task of retail merchandising can be executed through advertising and sales promotion functions.

In general, all of the activities and schemes which are designed to ultimately sell merchandise, increase store traffic, and create a favorable attitude toward the store fall into the category of advertising and sales promotion. Among such activities are setting up attractive in-store displays, preparing newspaper and other media advertising, sponsoring special fashion or other merchandise shows, and having salespersons furnish customers with advice and assistance when they come into the store. The objective of advertising and retail sales promotion is to *inform, invite, encourage,* and *persuade* potential customers to buy merchandise immediately or at some time in the future.

Planning the Promotional Tasks

The task of retail sales promotion is to communicate a message to prospective customers from the retail merchant, or between retail salespersons and the customers. The retail merchant can employ several different methods of executing this communication. The methods used are classified as either personal or non-personal. Personal communication is carried out face-to-face when the salesperson talks to the customer concerning product offerings. There is opportunity for exchange between salespersons and customers, and instant feedback can be obtained. In non-personal communication, however, there is no opportunity for face-to-face contact. This type of communication ranges from the supportive variety, such as in-store displays and special sale events, to retail advertising.

The ultimate objective of retail sales promotion is to generate sales profitably. Among the more specific objectives are (1) to sell specific goods immediately or in the short run, as when coupons are used; (2) to help create a desired store image, as in sponsoring the Little League; and (3) to help build store traffic on the ground that additional unplanned purchases will be made by customers attracted to the store by the promotional effort.

If retail promotion is to be effective, it cannot be left to chance. Each step must be carefully planned and executed. It is advisable that in planning the promotional task, the retail merchant should decide *what, why, how,* and *when* it is to be accomplished. If a new product line is being added and the principal task of selling it is assigned to promotion, selling 500 units the first week of introduction may be *what* is to be accomplished. To assist in boosting the overall store sales may be *why* this is to be accomplished. The *how* of accomplishment could be the use of effective, in-store displays and direct mail advertising. The setting of a deadline answers the question of *when* the goal of selling x number of units is to be attained. In addition, the cost of promotion must be considered in relation to its *reach* and expected sales results. The marginal sales volume generated by the promotion should exceed or at least equal the cost of the undertaking.

The method a retail merchant chooses to communicate with the prospective customer is a function of several factors, including the store's location, price of merchandise offered, store size, kind of merchandise sold, desired store image, season of the year, and age of the store. A single promotional method will rarely be adequate to get the job done. Several different methods which are compatible with one another may be employed at the same time to accomplish the objective.

The question of how much emphasis to place on promotion relative to other elements designed to help sell merchandise is quite important. If another element in the *retailing mix* such as price, for example, is particularly attractive to consumers, a store should not have to stress promotion as much as would another store which is not competitive on price.

The age of the retail establishment can influence the amount of emphasis that should be placed on promotion. In general, the beginning retail merchant has to stress promotion to a greater extent than the older, more established merchant. It is important for the beginning merchant to build customer patronage. Considerable advertising together with supplementary methods such as games, premiums, special sale events, and contests can be used to help attract the first-time customers. Salespeople are needed at this point to familiarize the customer with the store merchandise and services and to make the shopping trip more pleasant and rewarding. Following this, advertising and supplementary promotion may be employed so that first-time shoppers ultimately become repeat or regular customers.

Planning the Advertising Strategy

When properly planned and executed, advertising, together with other elements of retail merchandising, can be especially effective for the retail merchant. Through it, the aggressive merchant can create many opportunities to increase sales volume and profits. Carefully planned advertising efforts can be of significant value in building store traffic, a favorable image for the store, and a loyal customer following.

In contrast to a window display which is seen only by passersby and those who come to the store, advertising reaches beyond the store with a message, and it can be read by thousands of prospective customers. Advertising, including the print and broadcast media, is the primary method of communicating a message to target customers. Other kinds of retail promotion, such as in-store displays, stamps, games, and contests are considered secondary or supplementary methods of reaching target audiences. Because advertising is usually the dominant form of promotion, it is customary to allocate a larger proportion of the promotional budget to it. A retail merchant can either build goodwill through institutional advertising or generate a higher sales volume and profits through promotional advertising.

Institutional Advertising. The beginning retailer may wish to allocate some advertising dollars to promote the store itself. The "thing" featured in the advertising might be the name of the store, its location, services offered, or some other distinguishing characteristic. For example, a bookstore may stress the fact that it carries the largest number of titles in town.

Institutional advertising assumes various forms. The large merchants may stress the hugeness of their stores and emphasize such things as the variety of services offered and the broadness of their assortments. A store which sells fashion apparels may assume a leadership role through the periodic use of advertising which emphasizes the fact that it is the first in the area to stock new styles, that it carries exclusive brand names, and that it sponsors fashion shows. In institutional advertising, it is important to tell potential customers what they want and need to know about the store.

Promotional Advertising. Unlike institutional advertising, promotional advertising features specific products or services at identifiable prices to create immediate store traffic and sales volume. The beginning retail merchant might want to place great emphasis on this type of advertising to draw customers and to become known in the trading area. Different kinds of advertising are promotional in nature. First, there is regular promotional advertising which is designed to maintain the store traffic on a day-to-day basis, and it usually features merchandise at its regular markup prices. A second type of promotional advertising emphasizes price or some other kind of purchase inducements. Finally, there are *clearance* promotions, designed to dispose of slow-selling, shopworn, seasonal, or odd-lot merchandise. The major part of the advertising budget will go for promotional advertising rather than institutional advertising.

Advertising Expenditures

The beginning retail merchant should plan advertising expenditures as carefully as any other activities requiring an expenditure of funds. The major planning decisions involve determining the total advertising appropriation, timing the expenditures, and allocating the advertising appropriation to the different advertising media.

Planning the Total Appropriation. For the beginning retail merchant, the advertising appropriation may be based on a percentage of anticipated sales or on the objective and task method. In applying the percentage of anticipated sales method, the amount to be spent for advertising in the ensuing period is determined by multiplying the sales forecast by the percentage decided on. For example, if the sales forecast is $50,000 for the year ahead and if 4 percent of sales is to be appropriated for advertising, the amount to allocate would be $2,000 ($50,000 × 4%). In future periods, the percentage might be revised in light of the actual expenditures incurred and the net sales realized.

The objective and task method involves two steps. The first is to establish a reasonable sales goal for the store, which might be to increase sales by 10 percent next year. The second step is to determine what promotional effort is necessary to accomplish this objective. This might require that $500 be spent on radio advertising, $1,000 for newspaper advertising, $400 for direct mail pieces, and $100 for in-store displays, for a total of $2,000. When using this method, the amount of the appropriation is a function of the job to be accomplished.

Timing. Timing refers to a system of allocating the total advertising budget by months, weeks, or special promotion periods. For the beginning retail merchant, the total budget may be broken down to coincide with the anticipated monthly sales. For example, if net sales for the month of July are expected to amount to 5 percent of the annual sales, then approximately 5 percent of the total advertising budget would be spent on advertising during July. Once the sales distribution by months is obtained, the advertising appropriation can be allocated on about the same basis.

It may be advisable at times to deviate somewhat from the monthly sales distribution pattern. During months when the store is experiencing low sales volumes, it may be necessary to spend more of the advertising budget than what the sales percentage would indicate. This may be needed to maintain a minimum amount of market coverage. During the high sales volume months the advertising percentage may be less than the sales distribution percentage, especially if the season, such as Christmas or Easter, is a compelling reason for shopping. If 18 percent of the store's annual sales volume is made in December, spending 15 percent of the total advertising budget during this month may be quite adequate as people are motivated to buy due to the season of the year.

Planning the Advertising Media

For the retail merchant, advertising media offer certain advantages in reaching target customers with a message. They can be used individually or in combination for a possible greater impact on the listener or reader.

Newspapers. Newspapers are highly recommended as a medium in which to advertise. This is true for several reasons. First, newspapers provide comparatively wide market coverage for the merchant. Virtually every household in a store's trading area will get the daily newspaper, and newspapers are usually read by more than one member of the family. Second, the cost of reaching a household with a message is relatively low per newspaper reader. Third, newspapers afford a good opportunity for the merchant to use illustrations. Also, newspapers provide their clients with speed and flexibility. This means that an advertising message can often be run the day after submission to the paper, and that last minute changes can more easily be made in the content of the message.

Radio. Radio can be an effective advertising medium for the beginning retail merchant to use. Like newspapers, the radio is relatively inexpensive, and an advertising message can be aired in a short period of time following submission. It can reach an audience at any time—day or night—and at work or leisure. The radio provides sound, and it is flexible. Radio advertising, however, does not leave the listener with anything tangible which can be referred to as in the case of the print media.

Television. The retail merchant has the opportunity to expand business by advertising on television. Television can have a positive impact on the image of the store. Local retail merchants with branch stores and large merchants are in a better financial position to use television advertising. Because of the cost, advertising on television is not widely used by small retail merchants. The larger merchants who have several units operating in a given trading area can share the total cost of advertising with all of its stores in the area.

Direct Mail. The retail merchant can effectively use direct mail pieces to reach target customers. Direct mail advertising includes such devices as post cards, catalogs, letters, and booklets.
There are several reasons why direct mail advertising can be

particularly effective for the retail merchant. Direct mail enables the merchant to zero in on prospective customers or people who are considered to be good prospects. Direct mail messages are not in actual competition with other advertisers, as is the case with messages communicated by newspapers or radio. Direct mail can be personalized. The recipient can be addressed by name, which tends to have a great positive impact. Direct mail advertising is highly flexible. Direct mail is also recommended when a retail store wishes to communicate with its regular customers.

Deciding on What Promotional Tactics to Employ

There are a number of alternative promotional methods which retail merchants can employ to accomplish their objectives. These include special sale events, in-store displays, premiums and related patronage inducements, including games, contests, and trading stamps. These are supplementary to retail advertising, unless no advertising is used at all.

Special Sale Events. Progressive retail merchants can use special sales to their advantage. The major appeal used in the advertising to support a special sale may be price or value. Examples of special sales are January clearance sale, store anniversary sale, dollar day sale, and white goods sale. The purposes of the special sale are to stimulate the sale of regular merchandise, to sell promotional merchandise bought especially for the sale event, or to clear out seasonal, slower-selling, and broken assortment merchandise. While special sales are being conducted, it is important not to neglect the regular merchandise carried in stock.

In-Store Displays. The use of displays in the store may be one of the most important sales promotional tools that a beginning retail merchant can employ. In-store displays can be seen by customers while they are in the store and where the stimulation can elicit an immediate response from shoppers. Effective displays may be located in the store windows, near the main entrance, along the aisles, or near the cash registers.

The merchandise selected for display purposes should be carefully planned. It should be one of the store's best selling items. To sell readily, the merchandise must be attractive and appealing to a large number of customers. Some of the displays may be tied in with a strong national advertising campaign being carried on by a manufacturer who is the supplier. Also, some displays may aim at promoting the image of the store rather than to specifically sell merchandise immediately.

Premiums and Related Patronage Inducements. A premium is a tie-in arrangement in which a product or something else of value is offered free of charge, or at a discount, when a stipulated quantity of merchandise is purchased from the regular line. The premium would ordinarily not be part of the regular merchandise line. Premiums may be used to stimulate special sales or to promote patronage on a regular basis. A camera merchant may, for example, give customers two rolls of film free when they buy a new camera.

Games and Contests. A retail merchant can use games and contests as promotional tools for the store. The customer will participate in store games or contests to win cash, service, or merchandise as the prize. They are useful in building traffic for the store. Customers attracted to the store because of the game or contest are expected to do some shopping while they are in the store. As a consequence, the total store sales should increase, at least during the period that the game or contest is run.

Trading Stamps. Trading stamps may be effectively used as a form of retail sales promotion strategy by many different kinds of stores. Their effect on sales depends on the level of consumer interest in them, which tends to fluctuate over time. The retail merchant who participates in a stamp plan buys the stamps from a stamp company and issues them to their customers when they shop. The merchant might hand out stamps to shoppers at the rate of one for each ten cents worth of merchandise purchased. The stamps are then saved by customers. After accumulating the appropriate number of stamps, they are subsequently redeemed for prizes at redemption centers or stores.

Chapter Six

PLANNING AND CONTROLLING OPERATING EXPENSES

In generating sales revenue for a business, a retail merchant incurs operating expenses. These operating expenses are deducted from gross margin to arrive at the net profit (or loss). Unlike sales and the cost of sales which also affect net profit, some operating expenses are under the direct control of the owner/manager of the retail establishment. These should be planned and controlled to help improve the profitability of the store. Specifically, the owner/ manager must decide which expense items are avoidable and which are unavoidable. Salaries and wages, rent expense, taxes, and overhead costs are unavoidable. On the other hand, providing credit, delivery service, and check-cashing service are avoidable. It is the decision of the retail merchant whether or not to offer these avoidable services. In making the decision, the merchant should consider whether the services will generate enough additional sales revenue to pay for themselves.

Expense Budgeting

The expense budget is a tool which can be utilized to analyze and control retailing costs. It is a series of estimates of the various expense items together with the dollar amounts the store will incur during the operating period (which should coincide with the merchandise period).

The expense budget facilitates the planning of operating capital funds which will be needed during the period. It provides a basis for analyzing the extent of and reasons for any variations between the budgeted and the actual expenses incurred. For example, $5,000 is budgeted to cover the advertising expenses of a store for a six-month period, and the actual expenditures made for advertising for this period amounts to $5,500. An analysis of the situation may reveal that the $500 variation between the budgeted and actual cost can be explained by the fact that either the media cost was higher than planned or the merchant decided to run a $500 direct mail campaign in the middle of the budgeted period. The expense budget provides a means by which the retail merchant can analyze each expense item, or expense classification, after the actual expenditures are made.

To facilitate analysis at the end of the period, records of both budgeted and actual expenses should be maintained. At the conclusion of each budget period, the budgeted and actual amounts should be reviewed to ascertain whether any variations occurred and the reasons for them. In the case of supplies the following questions might be asked in an effort to uncover the reason for the variation: Why did the actual cost of supplies exceed the planned figure? Did the store use more wrapping paper and bags than was necessary? Was the budgeted figure unrealistic in light of unexpected developments? By seeking answers to these kinds of questions, the retail merchant obtains the information which is used as a basis for taking corrective action.

Expense *control* means taking action if necessary. A key advantage of the expense budget is that it permits the retail merchant to take early remedial action if it is warranted. A proposed expenditure for additional advertising in the middle of the period might be disallowed if it was not budgeted. Monthly reports which compare the actual expenses with the budgeted expenditures permit the merchant to monitor the expense trends. While the records which are maintained are not the control themselves, they are one step toward control. Control takes place when some kind of action is taken.

Expense Classification

In order for expenses to be analyzed and controlled, they must be classified in some manner. Certain industrywide classifications have been established, which if used make it possible for the beginning retail merchant to compare expenses with those of similar stores. The comparisons can be made only if all merchants classify their operating expenses in the same manner.

The Controllers Congress of the National Retail Merchants Association has evolved a system of expense classification and control which it refers to as *expense center accounting*. This system is based on the premise that each outlay of expenditure should be assigned to a category specific to the type of work which incurred the outlay. The expense centers are the categories or accounts which are selected to represent major areas of responsibility. The expense center system uses 23 expense accounts, each of which is descriptive of a major expense item.

Expense Centers

Management	Supplementary Benefits
Property and Equipment	Maintenance of Reserve Stock
Accounting and	Receiving and Marking
Data Processing	Shuttle Service
Accounts Receivable	Selling Supervision
Credit and Collections	Direct Selling
Sales Promotion	Customer Services
Service and Operations	Wrapping and Packing
Telephone and Other Utilities	Delivery
Cleaning	Merchandising
Maintenance and Repairs	Buying
Personnel	Merchandise Control

All of the expense centers are aggregates of controllable costs which are related to a particular type of work or service offered by a retail merchant. It is recommended that beginning merchants adopt this classification system of reporting expenses. This would facilitate the making of comparisons with other similar stores using the system. If sales promotion amounts to 0.5 percent of sales for one retail merchant at the end of a period, this could be compared with the industrywide percentage of similar type stores. This should be done for each of the expense accounts which apply. In cases where an expense percentage is greater than the industry average, a merchant needs to determine whether it is significant; if it is, the reasons for the overage should be explained. It might be that competition in the area was substantially more intense than the industry average and warranted more dollars for sales promotion in relation to sales than was indicated.

Allocation of Expenses

After a system for classifying expenses has been adopted, these expenses can then be distributed to the various selling departments in the store. If a beginning apparel merchant has three selling departments in the store, it is necessary to allocate indirect, or common, expenses among the three selling departments. This would be necessary in order to derive a net profit (or loss) for the period.

Some expenses would automatically be charged to each department because they were incurred by the department and would disappear if the department were closed. These are referred to as *direct expenses*. Direct expenses are salaries and wages of employees in the department, supplies used in the department, and the cost of advertising in a department. There are other types of expenses which cannot be automatically assigned to a department and would not disappear even if the department were to shut down. They are *indirect*, or *common expenses*, including rent for the entire store, heat and light, and taxes. There are two methods commonly used to allocate indirect expenses to the selling or revenue-producing departments of a store: (1) net profit method, and (2) contribution margin method.

The net profit method requires that all expenses, direct and indirect, be charged to each selling department or unit to arrive at the bottom line figure on the income statement. The bottom line figure is the net profit or loss. Since direct expenses originate in a particular department, they present no problem for the department. Indirect expenses, however, need to be assigned on a predetermined basis, such as by sales in a department, the amount of floor space occupied, number of invoices involved, or number of units delivered. Management expenses may be allocated to the various selling departments in ratio to sales in each department. Delivery expense may be charged to each department on the basis of the number of units or pieces delivered for each department. Maintenance and repairs expense may be allocated to each department according to sales or floor space occupied. Once the expenses have been allocated to the various selling departments, the net profit (or loss) can be calculated. All indirect expenses must be allocated when using the net profit method.

The contribution margin method allows a selling department to be judged on its contribution to profits and overhead. All direct expenses in the department are deducted from the departmental gross margin. But indirect expenses are not allocated or deducted. As a consequence, there is no net profit figure. Instead, there is a contribution margin or controllable margin. For example:

Net sales	$300,000
Cost of goods sold	200,000
Gross margin	$100,000
Direct expenses	70,000
Contribution margin (Controllable)	$ 30,000

Since there is no total expense figure with this method, no net profit (or loss) is determined. Hence, with the net profit method, all expenses must be absorbed, which requires the allocation of indirect expenses; with the contribution margin method, only the direct expenses apply, and there is no allocation requirement.

Chapter Seven

OTHER PLANNING ELEMENTS

In addition to the items covered in the preceding chapters which the beginning retail merchant must plan, other factors must also be considered. They are (1) what services, if any, to offer the customer, (2) what rate of return on capital funds invested in the store is desired, (3) what gross profit margin is desired, (4) the planned sales, (5) the planned purchases, and (6) the planned stock reductions, including markdowns, discounts to employees and special customers, and shortages.

Planning Customer Services

It is imperative for beginning retail merchants to carefully plan what services they will offer to their customers and how much emphasis to place on these services. A problem here for the beginning merchant is in determining what services customers expect or desire. In making this determination, the merchant's criterion may be to offer the services according to their importance to the customer.

There are services which provide convenience for the customer and are used by all shoppers. These include convenient shopping hours, attractive displays, adequate parking, effective sales help, convenient location, effective store layout and appearance.

Some services facilitate the sale of the merchandise directly. These services include credit, installation, delivery, and engraving. They may not be used by all customers, and whether they are used or not depends on the type of merchandise sold. Some sales cannot be made unless some of these services are provided. For example, some customers will not buy unless credit is available.

Some merchants might want to plan and offer certain auxiliary services: gift wrapping, layaways, accepting mail orders, accepting telephone orders, baby sitting, fashion consulting, or cashing checks. These services are promotional in nature and are, therefore, optional.

It is the responsibility of the retail merchant to decide which of the facilitating and auxiliary services to offer. Of course, the type of merchandise sold, i.e., durable goods as opposed to soft goods, will affect what services to offer. Other factors to consider are the needs of target customers, the kind of image the merchant wants to portray, the services which are offered by competitors, and the cost of providing the service.

Charging for Services. There are those store services which are never or seldom used by some customers. Some customers need delivery services, while others do not. Credit is highly desired by some customers, while others prefer to pay in cash. If the cost of the service is automatically included in the price of the merchandise, this means some customers would be paying for services they do not want or need. The beginning retail merchant must decide whether to offer these services free of charge to their customers, to charge all customers for them whether or not they are used, or to charge only the customers who use the service.

There is merit in charging customers only for the services they use. It means all customers would pay for the convenient services (directly or indirectly), while only those customers using the facilitating and auxiliary services would pay for them directly. It appears that it might be in the best long-run interest of the beginning retail merchant to provide all services which the store plans to offer free of charge, despite the fact that this might raise the prices of merchandise slightly.

Promoting Store Services. The beginning retail merchant should use services as a means of building store traffic or as institutional promotion. Customers need to be informed repeatedly about the services which the store offers. They need to know what benefits the store is providing on their behalf. Since services can be matched by competitors, it is important for beginning retail merchants to "sell" their services like any other merchandise they offer their customers. The quantity and quality of services offered is one way beginning merchants can differentiate their stores from competition.

Planning Profit and Return on Investment

Too often the retail merchant is negligent when it comes to planning and managing profits of the store. Instead of carefully planning profits, many merchants view them as residual, rather than as an item which can be planned and controlled throughout the year. Profits are a function of virtually every decision the merchant makes. But if profits are not carefully planned in advance, the merchant's decisions are not likely to result in consistent profits for the store.

Definitions of Profit. The word *profit* has different meanings to different retail merchants. Merchant Sanchez may define profit in terms of dollars of net profit after income taxes, or as the *bottom line* on the income statement. Merchant Brown might view profit in relation to sales, in which case profit will be stated as a percentage of sales. Merchant Segal may consider profit in relation to the amount of capital funds invested in the business to obtain that profit. Merchant Segal's view of profit is similar to the way a stock investor looks at the profit generated from the dollars invested in stocks, or the return earned from investing in another business. This type of investor is interested in what the stock returns on the investment (ROI).

Financial Goals. The retail merchant may also consider the financial goals of the business in terms of ROI. In order to generate a profit, the retail merchant must engage in a series of activities. The merchant's own capital, along with capital acquired from outside of the firm through loans and trade credit, is invested in the facilities, merchandise, operating capital, and other assets. The combination of these assets, together with personnel of the store, constitutes the total offerings of the store. If the *mix* is successful, the store will attract customers, generate sales, and produce a net profit, which becomes part of the business as owners' equity or net worth.

Now the retail merchant, like the financial investor, can analyze the net profit from the investment in the store. This is done in terms of the net profit produced by the store in relation to the investment required to get started and operate the store for a year. The retail merchant's financial objective may be expressed as:

$$\textbf{Return on investment} = \frac{\text{Net profit}}{\text{Capital invested}} \times 100$$

Return on investment may be calculated in two different ways, depending on how the term *investment* is defined. Investment can mean either *total assets*, the amount of investment in the business, or *net worth*, the total amount of the owners' investment. These two views of profitability are expressed as follows:

$$1. \ \ \textbf{Return on assets (ROA)} = \frac{\text{Net profit}}{\text{Total assets}} \times 100$$

$$2. \ \ \textbf{Return on net worth} = \frac{\text{Net profit}}{\text{Net worth}} \times 100$$

Return on assets is generally considered a measure of profitability for managers, because managers are expected to earn an adequate return on all funds invested in the business, whether the funds come from owners or creditors. Return on net worth is viewed as a measure of profitability from the standpoint of owners, or those who have supplied the store with the net worth funds.

It should be noted that return on net worth and return on assets are two concepts which are closely related. The relationship between these is:

Return on net worth = Return on assets × Financial leverage

$$\frac{\text{Net profit}}{\text{Net worth}} = \frac{\text{Net profit}}{\text{Total assets}} \times \frac{\text{Total assets}}{\text{Net worth}}$$

Net profit/total assets is the return on assets measurement, and it represents the amount of profit produced during the period for each dollar invested (by both owners and creditors) in the assets of the store. The total assets/net worth ratio is referred to as the *financial leverage* and is the dollar assets used in the business for each dollar in net worth, or owners' investment in the business. This means that if funds are borrowed from an outside source (bank or trade creditors), a retail merchant can obtain assets in excess of those supplied by the capital funds that the owners have invested in the business.

Furthermore, it can be seen that the net profit/total assets ratio is also the consequence of two factors: asset turnover and net profit margin.

Return on assets = Asset turnover × Net profit margin

$$\frac{\text{Net profit}}{\text{Total assets}} = \frac{\text{Net sales}}{\text{Total assets}} \times \frac{\text{Net profit}}{\text{Net sales}}$$

The first factor, net sales/total assets, is referred to as the rate of asset turnover, and it represents the dollar sales which are produced by each dollar of assets invested in the business. It is an indication of how much a merchant is getting from the assets used in the business. The second ratio, net profit/net sales, is the net profit margin, and it is the amount of net profit produced by each dollar in sales. It is a ratio of net profits to sales. All of these factors can be combined into a single equation to express the major elements in a retail merchant's financial standing:

$$\text{Return on net worth} = \text{Net profit margin} \times \text{Asset turnover} \times \text{Financial leverage}$$

$$\frac{\text{Net profit}}{\text{Net worth}} = \frac{\text{Net profit}}{\text{Net sales}} \times \frac{\text{Net sales}}{\text{Total assets}} \times \frac{\text{Total assets}}{\text{Net worth}}$$

To illustrate how the return on investment concept can be used to program retail profitability, study the data in the following hypothetical income statement and balance sheet and the return on net worth (RONW) equation which follows.

Income Statement	
Net sales	$200,000
Cost of goods sold	140,000
Gross margin	$ 60,000
Operating expenses	58,000
Net profit (before income taxes)	$ 2,000
Income taxes	1,000
Net profit (after taxes)	$ 1,000

Balance Sheet	
Current assets	$ 20,000
Fixed assets	30,000
Total assets	$ 50,000
Current liabilities	15,000
Fixed liabilities	20,000
Total liabilities	$ 35,000
Net worth	15,000
Total liabilities and net worth	$ 50,000

The return on net worth equation is as follows:

$$\textbf{RONW} = \frac{\text{Net profit}}{\text{Net sales}} \times \frac{\text{Net sales}}{\text{Total assets}} \times \frac{\text{Total assets}}{\text{Net worth}}$$

The appropriate data from the income statement and balance sheet are substituted in the equation to derive the return on net worth.

$$\frac{\$\ 1,000}{\$15,000} = \frac{\$\ 1,000}{\$200,000} \times \frac{\$200,000}{\$\ 50,000} \times \frac{\$50,000}{\$15,000}$$
$$6.7\% = .5\% \times 4.0 \times 3.3$$

The retail merchant may decide that the 6.7 percent return on net worth after taxes is inadequate, and that a 10 percent return on net worth will be the target for the next year. The merchant will, therefore, want to develop a merchandising plan for the next year which will produce a higher rate of inventory turnover and a higher gross margin percent, improving the store's overall profitability.

In developing such a plan, the merchant should start with an overall financial objective of 10 percent return on net worth. To achieve the target RONW of 10 percent while maintaining the store's present financial leverage ratio of 4.0, the return on assets (ROA) will have to increase from the present 2 percent ($1,000/$50,000) to 3.03 percent:

$$\textbf{RONW} = \text{ROA} \times \text{Financial leverage ratio}$$
$$10\% = \text{ROA} \times 3.3$$

Therefore,

$$\text{ROA} = \frac{10\%}{3.3} = 3.03\%$$

It is vitally important for the retail merchant to plan and carry out these steps to achieve the desired financial goals.

Planning the Gross Margin

The term *gross margin*, sometimes called *gross profit* or *gross margin of profit*, is defined as the difference in dollars between the total cost of goods sold and net sales. If there are workroom costs or cash discounts taken on merchandise purchased, they must be taken into consideration in computing the total cost of goods sold. The relationship can be expressed as:

$$\text{Total cost of goods sold} = \text{Gross cost of goods sold} + \text{Workroom cost} - \text{Cash discounts}$$

Also,

$$\textbf{Gross margin} = \text{Net sales} - \text{Total cost of goods sold}$$

If neither workroom costs nor cash discounts are applicable for a particular merchant, then the total cost of goods sold and the gross cost of goods sold will be the same.

The gross margin can also be determined by making an adjustment in the maintained markup, which is the difference between the gross cost of goods sold and the net sales. The case discounts would be added to the maintained markup, and the net workroom costs would be deducted.

$$\textbf{Gross margin} = \text{Maintained markup} + \text{Cash discounts} - \text{Net workroom costs}$$

The reason for this kind of adjustment is illustrated next. Assume that an apparel merchant purchases 300 coats at a cost of $3,600, $12 each, and prices them to retail at $7,200, or $24 each. The initial markup on each coat is $12, and the cumulative markon is $3,600. Assume further than 150 are sold at the original retail price of $24; that 50 are marked down and sold at $20 each; and the remaining 100 are marked down and sold at $16 each, for a total net sales of $6,200. Related to this special order of coats are alterations which cost the store $2 a coat, bringing the total workroom cost to $600. In addition, a 2 percent cash discount was earned on the purchase of coats which amounts to $72 ($3,600 × 0.02). These relationships are shown by using both the *cost of goods sold* approach, and the *maintained markup* approach. Using the cost of goods sold approach, the relationships are as follows:

Sales	$7,200
Less: Gross cost of goods sold	− 3,600
Add: Workroom costs	+ 600
Deduct: Cash discounts	− 72
Total cost of goods sold	$4,128
Gross margin	$2,072

Using the maintained markup approach, the relationships are expressed in the following manner:

Sales	$7,200
Less: Cost of goods sold	− 3,600
Maintained markup	$2,600
Add: Cash discounts earned	+ 72
Deduct: Workroom costs	− 600
Gross margin	$3,072

In some cases, the cash discounts earned will exceed the alteration costs, particularly if some of the alteration costs are paid by the customers. Whenever this is the case, the gross margin is greater than maintained markup.

When there are no workroom costs or cash discounts involved, gross margin and maintained markup will be identical. In stores which do not stock apparels, there are usually no alterations or workoom costs. There are also some apparel shops which sell ready-to-wear clothing but do not make alterations for their customers. Also, in some instances, the supplier offers no cash discounts, or the retail merchant may fail to take advantage of any possible cash discount.

Planning Sales

The retail merchant should plan the sales that are expected in the year ahead, because the amount of merchandise to be purchased depends on the expected sales for the period. The sales planning procedure involves estimating the season's needs and then dividing up the total estimate into months or weeks. The sales estimate is usually expressed in terms of dollars rather than in units.

In developing a sales forecast, the usual starting point is to review past sales, particularly those of the immediate past year. When compared with other years, it may give some indication of a trend for the coming year. For the beginning retail merchant, however, there are no past sales records on which to base future estimates. The sales figures of other similar stores in the trading area could be used as a base and adjusted to reflect the specific environmental conditions of the store. Also, average sales figures of past years for similar types and sizes of stores which could be used as a base may be obtained from trade publications. These data would then be adjusted to fit local conditions in the trading area of the store.

It is possible to plan sales by starting with the development of a number of minute forecasts by brands, product lines, price lines, or departments. These unit forecasts are then evaluated in light of specific environmental conditions, including competition. Based on the review, any necessary adjustments are then made. Finally, all the unit forecasts are added together to develop a forecast for the store as a whole.

In the process of developing the sales forecast or estimates, there are several factors to consider which might be useful in increasing the accuracy of the sales estimate. First, the extent to which advertising and promotion will be emphasized during the year will impact on sales. A retail merchant who plans to spend an above-average amount on advertising and promotion would adjust the forecast slightly upward. Second, the extent of the proposed services to be provided may affect the sales volume. If the quality of the services to be offered is clearly superior to the competitions', this may warrant a higher than average sales forecast. Third, the extent to which other similar merchants in the trading area are aggressive should be considered. If the beginning merchant plans to be considerably more aggressive in merchandising than other merchants with similar stores in the area, this would also warrant a more optimistic sales forecast for the year.

Planning the Stock Reductions

It is important to plan stock reductions so that sales and profit goals can be more accurately reached. The amount of the expected reductions should be reflected in the initial markup percent on merchandise bought by the store. If it is not included in the calculation of the initial markup, the markup percentage will be inadequate to achieve the desired profit goal. Stock reductions are also needed when purchases are being planned. This is because if the planned purchases figure does not include the expected reductions, the amount of purchases made for a period will be inadequate to meet consumer demand and the planned end-of-month stock requirements. Retail reductions include markdowns, stock shortages, and discounts to employees and special customers.

Markdowns. Markdowns are the most important type of price adjustments a retail merchant can make. They are reductions in the original or previous retail price of an item. When markdowns are taken, the amount of gross profit a store earns is correspondingly reduced. A vase which costs $50 was initially priced to retail at $100. It is marked down to $90 and sold. The gross profit on the vase would be $40, versus $50 if the markdown had not been taken. The net profit amount the store would have realized will likewise be reduced by the extent of the markdowns taken.

There are several reasons why retail merchants will want to take markdowns. Mistakes in buying and pricing may have been made. Some of the merchandise bought for the store may not be exactly what the store's customers want and it does not sell at the original retail price. Markdowns may be taken on merchandise to make some promotional or sale merchandise available. Some markdowns may have to be taken to sell surplus or overbought merchandise—consumer demand may have been overestimated. Markdowns are also necessary in order to sell odds and ends which have accumulated in the merchandise inventory. These would be the irregular sizes and unusual colors which are in less demand. Finally, merchandise which has been excessively handled by customers and merchandise returned to the store by customers for various reasons cannot be sold at the original retail price.

Planned markdowns are usually expressed in both dollar and percentage terms. The markdown percentage is the ratio of the dollar markdowns to the net sales for that period. A fur coat which had an original retail price of $5,000 was marked down by $1,000 and sold. The markdown percentage is calculated as follows:

$$\textbf{Markdown \%} = \frac{\$ \text{ markdown}}{\$ \text{ net sales}}$$

Substituting,

$$\text{Markdown \%} = \frac{\$1,000}{\$5,000 - \$1,000}$$
$$= \frac{\$1,000}{\$4,000}$$
$$= 0.25 \text{ or } 25\%$$

It should be noted that markdown percentages are based on the net selling price (the actual selling price, or selling price after markdowns are taken). A markdown percentage can also be stated in terms of the original retail price. When this is the case, it is referred to as *off-retail* percentage. The off-retail percentage can be calculated as follows:

$$\textbf{Off-retail \%} = \frac{\$ \text{ markdown}}{\text{Original retail price of goods marked down}}$$

Using the preceding amounts and substituting in this equation, off-retail percent equals ($1,000/$5,000), or 20 percent. (Note that when the dollar markdown is based on the net selling price, it yields a larger percent than when it is based on the original retail price.) The retail merchant might want to use the off-retail percentage to advertise to the general public when clearance sales are being conducted by the store. The ad might read, "All Summer Swimming Wear Reduced 20 Percent."

The timing of markdowns can be critically important. If markdowns are taken early in the selling period, this would clear out space in the store which could then be used for fresh and faster-selling merchandise. Also, the merchant who takes early markdowns can usually move the affected merchandise with smaller markdowns than would be required later on in the season. But late markdowns can give "late blooming" merchandise a chance to catch on with customers and possibly sell at the higher original price. If markdowns must be taken late in the season, they generally must be larger in order to sell the merchandise than if they were taken early in the season.

It is possible to adopt an automatic markdown policy. This means that when an item is unsold after a certain length of time, it is automatically reduced by a specified amount; if it does not sell at the reduced price within another specified interval of time, additional predetermined markdowns are taken.

The amount of the markdown should be just large enough to interest consumers in buying the unsold merchandise. The percentage markdown a merchant should take depends upon such factors as the cost of the unsold merchandise, how badly the merchant needs the funds which are tied up in the stock, and how late it is in the season before the markdown is taken. In general, the higher the cost of the merchandise, the larger the markdown that would ordinarily be taken. If a retail merchant needs funds desperately, a larger markdown may be warranted to get a faster turnover of the merchandise. Finally, if a markdown is taken at the end of the selling season, it is considerably larger than markdowns taken early in the season.

Discounts to Employees and Customers. Discounts to employees and special customers represent price adjustments which should be considered by merchants, because they also affect the initial markup percentage and the quantity of goods purchased during the period. These discounts are called retail reductions because they result in deductions from the original price. Except for stores in the food business selling groceries, most retail merchants give discounts to their employees. The size of the discounts vary, but a 10 percent discount is quite common.

Discounts are usually given to customers who occupy a special status in the eyes of the merchant. A bookstore may give teachers a discount on purchases made; an automobile parts merchant may give automobile mechanics a discount on parts; and a camera shop could offer professional photographers a discount on equipment and supplies purchased. Special discounts may be given to churches, schools, charitable organizations, senior citizens, and members of the clergy. These kinds of discounts represent a reduction in price just as markdowns do.

Stock Shortages. A third kind of retail reduction that should be considered in planning the markup percentage and purchases are stock shortages. Shortages are caused by any shrinkage in the value of the merchandise inventory, which is attributable to several factors. Theft is a principle cause of stock shortage and entails shoplifting by customers and pilferage by the store employees. Stock shortages can be due to a physical loss as in a loss in weight of products sold by the pound. Some items which are not sold in standardized packages may be mismeasured or incorrectly weighed (to the detriment of the store). Finally, clerical errors may incorrectly indicate a stock shortage or overage.

When the books are maintained on sales, markdowns, employee discounts, and returns to suppliers the amount of the stock shortage can be calculated at the end of the period. This is done by comparing the *book* inventory figure (the amount of stock that should be on hand according to the records) with the *actual* inventory (the amount of stock on hand at the end of the period according to the actual physical count). When the book inventory figure is larger than the actual inventory (the usual case), the differential is called a *shortage;* when it is smaller, the differential is an *overage.* An overage is caused by an error in bookkeeping.

In order to reduce stock shortages, a number of steps may be taken. The retail merchant may set up certain physical safeguards, such as keeping the display cases locked to protect the merchandise. To detect and discourage thievery, an electronic surveillance system could be installed whereby customers are observed while they are shopping. Carefully trained salespeople can be most important in discouraging shoplifting. Various checks and controls should be installed at the receiving and marking stations in the store. The blind check could be used for incoming merchandise. This method requires listing each arriving order by describing the merchandise, the quantity, the shipper, etc., of the shipment. The checker does not have access to the invoice or purchase order and, therefore, does not know exactly what is expected.

Planning the Purchases

Once a decision has been made relative to *what* to buy for the store, the beginning merchant needs to know *how much* to buy, which is critical for the overall success of the store. Even if a merchant buys the right merchandise, the wrong quantity can pose a serious problem.

The amount of merchandise a beginning merchant needs during a particular merchandise planning period is a function of planned sales for the period, the amount of planned reductions in the inventory that will take place, and the value of the merchandise inventory the merchant will want to have on hand at the end of the period. In arriving at planned purchases, these three elements are simply added together. Hence, the following is the formula for ascertaining planned purchases.

Planned purchases (at retail) = Planned sales + Planned reductions + Planned end of the month stock*

In Belle's Dress Shop, planned sales for the month are $12,000, planned reductions are $1,000, and the end of the month stock is planned at $14,000. The amount of purchases to be made during the period can be calculated as follows:

$$\text{Planned purchases} = \$12,000 + \$1,000 + \$14,000$$
$$= \$27,000 \text{ (at retail value)}$$

Note that the $27,000 of planned purchases for the period is at retail value. It is not the dollar amount the beginning merchant can spend on merchandise during the period. Because it is at retail, it has to be converted to its *cost equivalent*, which is the amount that can be spent. The cost equivalent is obtained by multiplying the retail figure by the *cost complement* (100 percent − the initial markup percent) of the planned initial markup percent. In this case, if the initial markup is 36 percent of the original retail price, the cost equivalent is $7,040 [$11,000 × (100% − 36%)], which is the dollar amount that the retail merchant can use to make purchases for the store.

The amount to be purchased for a month or any merchandise planning period does not limit the placing of orders to that month. Some orders which are needed in the month of May might be placed in May; others might have been placed in April or perhaps earlier, depending on the amount of *lead* time that is needed. The timing of orders in a particular case is a function of such factors as the distance between the store and the suppliers, the amount of time needed to process an order, whether the merchandise is bought from the supplier's stock or by specification, and the method by which the items are transported to the store.

---

* The stock on hand at the end of the first period becomes the beginning of period stock for the next period. When there is a beginning period stock, it is a deduction in the planned purchases formula because it is stock which is already on hand.

Summary

In planning the assortment needs of the store, the beginning merchant should consider depth, breadth, and consistency in the assortment mix. The assortment should be planned by keeping in mind the type of customers the merchant wants to cultivate and merchandise to.

Open-to-buy is an important device for controlling the amount of stock the store can buy during the remaining part of a merchandise planning period. It can be quite useful in enabling the merchant to stay within a budget.

To help improve the stock turn rate and overall store profitability, the merchandise inventory should be carefully planned and controlled. Some tools which can be used to facilitate stock planning and control include the setting up of stock classifications, planning in both dollar and unit terms, and maintaining the records of the business on either a perpetual or periodic basis.

The stock-sales ratio method or weeks-of-supply method might be used to help plan stock that should be on hand or to support a given expected sales volume at the beginning of the month.

The merchant should be interested in the rate at which the stock turns. On a unit basis, a ratio of 3.0 means the individual item sold three times during the year. The merchant will want to have a reasonable turn rate in relation to the type of merchandise sold. A high turnover rate helps to ensure fresh merchandise, reduce investment in inventory, and free up funds for unexpected buys.

In order to maintain a healthy cash flow position, the beginning merchant should carefully plan and control the inflow and outlay of cash. The forecasting of cash receipts and cash disbursements makes it possible to have adequate funds on hand to meet operating needs from internal and outside sources of funds.

The interior layout of the store can serve an important merchandising function for the merchant. The type of layout arrangement used will be influenced by the size and shape of the store, type of merchandise sold, selling methods used, fixtures and equipment used, and the customer traffic patterns.

The merchandise for sale should be placed at locations in the store for maximum impact on sales. Space ordinarily allocated to departments or product lines should be based on the productivity of the department or unit, in terms of sales in relation to the amount of space occupied. Exceptions can be made for items requiring special treatment, such as bulky items.

The prices charged by beginning merchants tend to impact on all aspects of merchandising, including the image of the store. Setting the right prices can be critically important in generating sales revenue and profits. To realize profit goals, the initial markup price placed on incoming merchandise should take into account operating expenses and retail reductions, including expected markdowns, stock shortages, and discounts to employees and special customers.

A carefully planned and executed advertising and promotional campaign should be of significant value in helping beginning merchants attain their sales and profit goals. Advertising informs, invites, persuades, and encourages prospective customers to buy, while retail promotion is usually concerned principally with getting immediate sales. For greater impact, several advertising media might be employed at any one time, supplemented by promotionals such as in-store displays.

In order to plan and meet profit goals, it is important to plan and control the operating expenses which will be incurred during the year by the beginning merchant. One way of controlling the operating expenses is to set up an expense budget. To facilitate analysis of expenses at the end of the year and to make comparisons with other similar merchants, it is imperative merchants classify their expenses like other similar stores. If there are several departments in the store, each serving as an individual profit center, it is necessary that indirect expenses be allocated so that a net profit figure can be derived for each revenue-producing department or unit. Finally, the beginning merchant should also plan such things as what customer services to offer, return on inventory investment, sales, stock reductions, and purchases.